Awater

from the Ret, Cat
and Mac! xxxx

± 4

Martinus Nijhoff

Awater

Edited by Thomas Möhlmann

with an essay by Wiljan van den Akker

Translations by

David Colmer
James S. Holmes
Daan van der Vat

Ânwater
Nighhoff

Anvil Press Poetry

Published in 2010
by Anvil Press Poetry Ltd
Neptune House 70 Royal Hill London SE10 8RF
www.anvilpresspoetry.com

This book is published with financial assistance
from Arts Council England
and the Dutch Foundation for Literature

Designed and set in Monotype Bembo by Anvil
Printed and bound in Great Britain
by Hobbs the Printers Ltd

ISBN 978 0 85646 407 2

Contents

Acknowledgements

Daan van der Vat's translation was first published in Miron Grindea's *Adam* no. 196, 1949, and is here reprinted in the slightly revised version from *De Gids*, Vol. 117, No. 2 (February 1954), pp. 117–125, where it follows the Dutch original of his '*Awater* in English' (pp. 110–117). James S. Holmes's translation is reprinted from *Delta: A Review of Arts Life and Thought in the Netherlands*, Volume IV, No. 2 (Summer 1961) and *Modern Poetry in Translation*, nos. 27–8, 1976. His English translation of excerpts from Nijhoff's Enschede lecture is from the same issue of *Delta*. Thomas Möhlmann's preface is based on an article published in the yearbook *The Low Countries*, no. 17, 2009.

We thank the Dutch Foundation for Literature and its former incarnation, the Foundation for the Production and Translation of Dutch Literature, for its constant support for this book.

Preface

THOMAS MÖHLMANN

Two gentlemen in a restaurant in Nijmegen. During dinner one of them says with a sigh what a shame it is to write poetry in a language that reaches so few people as Dutch does. This means that his audience remains some-what limited, and that weighs on his heart. Eventually the other man promises to go home and not rest until he has translated one of his friend's major works into English. According to his own account, that is how poet and translator Daan van der Vat embarked on the first English translation of Martinus Nijhoff's *Awater* in 1939. Van der Vat completed a first version in three days, and then spent the next ten years honing the translation. During this time face-to-face contact was hampered by, among other things, the German occupation and Van der Vat's emigra-tion to London, but nonetheless poet and translator discussed the progress and finer points of the translation from time to time by letter.

Martinus Nijhoff was born in The Hague in 1894, into a family of booksellers and publishers. He studied law in Amsterdam and – much later – literature in Utrecht. During his life he published four collections of poetry, which belong to the best work ever published in Dutch. Right from his debut with *De wandelaar* (The Wanderer) in 1916, he was recognized as a poet of rare brilliance. In the 1920s he became an editor of the prominent literary review *De Gids*, and a critic for the daily newspapers *Het Nieuws van den Dag* and *Nieuwe Rotterdamsche Courant*. His next collections, *Vormen* (Forms) in 1924 and *Nieuwe gedichten* (New Poems) in 1934, confirmed his reputation as a great innovator of the Dutch literary landscape, although he remained faithful to traditional verse forms. His last important work of poetry was the long poem *Het uur U* (H-Hour, or Zero Hour), which was published in conjunction with *Een Idylle* (An Idylle) in 1942. After that, he mainly dedicated himself to writing plays and translations, until his untimely death in 1953.

The long poem *Awater*, which appeared in 1934 as part of *Nieuwe gedichten*, is indisputably one of Nijhoff's most important works, which immediately makes it also one of the most important works in twentieth-century Dutch poetry. The modern and startling atmosphere, the stylistic refinement, the network of allusions and references, the concrete meanings and their various possible interpretations: whole books have been written about these features in the Netherlands, literary reputations built on them, readers bewitched by them and poets inspired by them to this very day. Of course this does not relate to *Awater* alone: it relates to Nijhoff's poetry and his views on poetry in general. It is precisely for this reason that Nijhoff's lament at the limited reach of Dutch is still so understandable. Apparently T. S. Eliot, whom Nijhoff admired, said after reading *Awater* that if he only had written it in English rather than Dutch, Nijhoff would have been world-famous. And another Nobel Prize winner, Joseph Brodsky, referred to *Awater* as 'one of the grandest works of poetry in this century', and added: 'It's a completely different thing. This is the future of poetry, I think, or it at least paves the way for a very interesting future.'

Meanwhile, Nijhoff's work has been translated into about fifteen languages, and in some countries – such as

Slovenia, Germany and Russia – not just in a general anthology or periodical but as a fully-fledged Selected Poems. But still: our greatest twentieth-century poet is not yet really world-famous. And while in recent years contemporary Dutch-language poets have been able to enjoy increasing attention and appreciation abroad, it would be good if the world beyond our borders could also be given a fuller picture of the work of their most important forerunners, such as Nijhoff. As regards *Awater* in England, Van der Vat's first step, the original translation initiative, was followed by a second: in 1949 he finally published his translation in the London periodical *Adam*. A good ten years later a second translator, this time a native English speaker, ventured to tackle Nijhoff's masterpiece: the Netherlands-based American James S. Holmes. The new translation, published in 1961 in the periodical *Delta*, was highly praised and seemed so to impress everyone that for a long time not a single other translator attempted to surpass him. It has taken until the twenty-first century for the Australian author and translator David Colmer to take up the challenge, at the request of the Foundation for the Production and Translation of Dutch Literature. His approach is not only fresh and contemporary, it is also ambitious. His aim is to achieve something that both previous translators had failed to do: not only to be semantically and metrically (at least reasonably) faithful but also to reflect the rich assonances of the original verse in a better way in the translation. In this way Colmer has possibly come a bit closer still to what is the ideal for many translators of poetry: to create a translation that is as much a poem in its own right in the target language as the original poem is in the source language.

The English public will now be able to compare the existing *Awater* translations for itself. In this book the three translations are given in reverse chronological order, from 2009 to 1961 to 1949, preceded by the Dutch original. Daan van der Vat's account of his translation's interrupted progress quotes from his correspondence with Nijhoff between 1939 and 1949. Two other accounts by translators – a brief one by James S. Holmes, a fuller one by David Colmer – are followed by Holmes's translation of passages from Nijhoff's famous 'Enschede lecture', given to the Enschede Folk University in 1935, a year after the completion of *Awater*. The text of this lecture was not published during the poet's lifetime; the passages included, those most closely having to do with the genesis of *Awater*, are from a draft found among his papers. In the lecture he explains how *Awater* came about, and sets the poem and his poetic vision against the background of his times. The title of the lecture alone, 'Poetry in a Period of Crisis', indicates that Nijhoff's poetry, and also his thinking *about* poetry, have still lost little of their topicality. Finally, the essay by the Dutch Nijhoff expert, Wiljan van den Akker, discusses the poem in the context of international modernism, illuminating key elements of the poem and Nijhoff's craft.

Some sixty years after *Awater* could first be read in England in a periodical, Martinus Nijhoff finally gets what he had always wanted – and deserved: his first English volume. We must hope – and expect – that it will not be another sixty years before somebody takes the next step and publishes a more comprehensive Nijhoff anthology in English.

Translated by Sheila Dale

Awater

MARTINUS NIJHOFF

'ik zoek een reisgenoot'

Wees hier aanwezig, allereerste geest,
die over wateren van aanvang zweeft.
Uw goede oog moet zich dit werk toe keren,
het is gelijk de wereld woest en leeg.
Het wil niet, als geheel een vorige eeuw,
puinhopen zien en zingen van mooi weer,
want zingen is slechts hartstocht van een zweer
en nimmer is, wat ook, ooit puin geweest.
Een eerste steen ligt nauwelijks terneer.
Elk woord vernieuwt de stilte die het breekt.
Al wat geschiedt geschiedt nog voor het eerst.
Geprezen! Noach bouwt, maar geen ark meer,
En Jonas preekt, maar niet te Ninive.

Ik heb een man gezien. Hij heeft geen naam.
Geef hem ons aller vóórnaam bij elkaar.
Hij is de zoon van een vrouw en een vader.
Zodra de rode zon is opgegaan
gaat hij de stad in. Hij komt langs mijn raam.

De avond blauwt, hij komt er weer vandaan.
Hij werkt op een kantoor, heet daar Awater.
Zie hem. Hij is bekleed met kemelhaar
geregen door een naald. Zijn lijf is mager
gespijsd met wilde honing en sprinkhanen.
Niemand heeft ooit hetgeen hij roept verstaan.
Het is woestijn waar hij gebaren maakt.
Hij heeft iets van een monnik, een soldaat,
maar er wordt niet gebeden, niet geblazen,
wanneer men op kantoor het boek opslaat.
Men zit als in een tempel aan een tafel.
Men schrijft Arabisch schrift met Italiaans.
In cijfers, dwarrelend als as omlaag,
rijzen kolommen van orakeltaal.
Het wordt stil, het wordt warmer in de zaal.
Steeds zilter waait dun ratelend metaal.
De schrijfmachine mijmert gekkenpraat.
Lees maar, er staat niet wat er staat. Er staat:
'O moeder, nooit zult gij de bontjas dragen
waarvoor elk dubbeltje werd omgedraaid,
en niet meer ga ik op mijn vrije dagen
met een paar bloemen naar het hospitaal,
maar breng de rozen naar de Kerkhoflaan . . .'
Dit staat er, en Awaters strak gelaat
geeft roerloos zijn ontroering te verstaan.
Hoe laat is het? Awaters hoofd voelt zwaar.
De telefoon slaapt op de lessenaar.
De theekopjes worden teruggehaald.

De klok tikt, tikt, slaat, tikt tot halfzes slaat.
De groene lampen worden uitgedraaid.

Vandaag, toen ik voor 't raam de bloemen goot,
is het voornemen in mij opgekomen
Awater te gaan halen van kantoor.
Ik heb sinds mijn broer stierf geen reisgenoot.
Als men een vriend zoekt, is het doodgewoon
dat men eerst ziet of men bij hem kan horen.
Vanavond volg ik dus Awaters spoor,
ik kijk de kat, zo men zegt, uit de boom,
en morgen, gaat het goed, stel ik mij voor.
Zo sta ik bij de hoge stoep. Ik schroom.
Het slaat halfzes. De tijd wordt eindeloos.
De straat wordt door voorbijgangers doorstroomd.
In elke schaduw wordt een licht ontstoken,
makend, al dwalend, omtrekken in rook.
O broeder in de hemel, wees hier ook.
Bescherm mij, dat mijn schim geen licht vertoont.
Bewaar mij ongezien en ongehoord. –
Opeens Awater. Van een overloop
zie ik hem komen, knipperend met 't oog.
Geen sterveling, geen stad, geen avondrood
bestaat voor hem. Hij komt gesneld van boven,
zandstenen trappen af langs slangen koper.
Hij ziet, schijnt het, een horizon, een zoom
waaruit ononderbroken weerlicht gloort.
Het is alsof hij hoort waarvan hij droomt

en de plek ziet waar hij te vinden hoopt,
zo snelt hij langs me, en ik voel mij doorboord.
Hij loopt haastig de vestibule door.
Hij hangt een sleutel op het sleutelboord.
Een droge distel doet zich aan hem voor,
hij grijpt zijn stok, hij wandelt fluitend voort.
Hij dekt zich, ik echter ontbloot het hoofd:
Wees hier, nogmaals, gij die op hoogten woont
zo onbewoonbaar als Calvario.

De straten zijn met asfalt geplaveid.
Ik merk dat de echo, die mij uitgeleide
deed door de hall met tegels, buiten zwijgt.
De stad verleent de voet geluidloosheid.
Een rij auto's glijdt karavaansgewijs
met zacht gekraak van leer aan ons voorbij.
Awater is mij reeds vooruitgeijld.
Ja, ja, 't schijnt waar te zijn, hij wil op reis.
Hij staat stil voor het modemagazijn.
Ik zie dat hij naar een gezelschap kijkt
van poppen die met plaids en verrekijkers
legeren aan de oever van de Nijl
gelijk uit piramide en palmboom blijkt.
O Awater, ik weet waarvan gij peinst,
iets verder, bij de plaat der scheepvaartlijn
waarop een bedoeïen in de woestijn
een schip begroet dat over zee verschijnt,
en, weer iets verder, bij het bankpaleis

waar 'vreemd geld' genoteerd staat in de lijst.
Zo gaan wij samen langs de winkelschijnsels.
Eensklaps is hij verdwenen in een zijstraat.
Een deurbel klinkt. Daar moet hij binnen zijn.
Er staat geschreven: scheren en haarsnijden.
Het klein vertrek met kasten aan weerszij
lijkt door de sterke geur van allerlei
parfumerieartikelen nog kleiner.
Awater – ik moet zeggen, ik ben blij
dat ik hem zie, ik was hem bijna kwijt, –
zit in een mantel van gesteven lijnwaad
voor de wastafel van wit porselein.
De kapper doet zijn werk, en ik zet mij
als wie zijn beurt wacht, op een stoel terzijde.
Nooit zag ik Awater zo van nabij
als thans, via de spiegel; nooit scheen hij
zo nimmer te bereiken tegelijk.
Tussen de flessen, glinsterend verbrijzeld,
verrijst hij in de spiegel als een ijsberg
waarlangs de gladde schaar zijn snavel strijkt.
Maar het wordt lente, en terwijl wijd en zijd
de damp hangt van een bui die overdrijft
ploegt door het woelend haar de kam de scheiding.
Dan neemt Awater van de kapper afscheid
en ik volg hem op straat, werktuigelijk.

Het toeval neemt een binnenweg naar 't doel.
Moest het, dat Awater belanden moest

in het café waar ik kwam met mijn broer?
Het moest, en hij zit zelfs in onze hoek.
Ik zet mij ergens anders. Plaats genoeg.
De kelner kent me. Hij weet wat ik voel.
Hij heeft mijn tafeltje al tweemaal gepoetst.
Hij blijft, met in zijn hand de witte doek,
geruime tijd staan zwijgen naast mijn stoel.
'De tijden' zegt hij 'zijn niet meer als vroeger.'
Ik weet dat hij ook aan mijn broer denkt, hoe
met zijn hond aan de ketting en zijn hoed
iets achterover op, hij binnenwoei
en 't hele zaaltje vulde met rumoer.
Hier ligt hetzelfde zand nog op de vloer,
dezelfde duif koert in zijn kooi als toen.
Oei, zei de wind, voort, voort! Zo is het goed.
Wie is dat? zeg ik daar 'k iets zeggen moet.
En hij, wetend terstond op wie ik doel:
'Iemand die voor het eerst de zaak bezoekt.'
Dan trekt hij van 't buffet het hekje toe.
In 't water worden glazen omgespoeld. –
Wat is 't dat in zijn zak Awater zoekt?
Het is een boekje van marokko groen.
Het is een schaakspel nu hij 't opendoet.
Awaters ogen kijken koel en stroef.
Zijn hand, op tafel trommelend, schenkt moed
aan het visioen dat door zijn voorhoofd woelt.
Een sneeuwvlok dwarrelt tussen droppen bloed.
Het spel wordt tot een nieuw figuur gevoegd.

Zijn glas, vóór hem, beslaat onaangeroerd.
De sigaret die in de asbak gloeit
maakt een stokroos die langs 't plafond ontbloeit.
Hij zit volstrekt alleen en ongemoeid.
Hij heeft wat een planeet heeft en een bloem,
een innerlijke vaart die diep vervoert.
Nu drinkt hij het glas leeg en sluit het boek.
Hij krijgt, nu hij stil voor zich kijkt, iets droevigs.
Hij kijkt mijn kant uit, zodat ik vermoed
dat hij mij roept als hij de kelner roept.
Maar neen, hij rekent af, ik ook, en spoedig
gaan wij weer samen door het straatgewoel.

Elektrisch licht dat langs de gevel schiet
schrijft ieder ogenblik de naam opnieuw
van 't restaurant, en een dubbele file
mensen gaat in en uit langs de portier
die de toegang van draaiend glas bedient.
Terwijl wij binnentreden klinkt muziek.
Awater blijkt bekendheid te genieten.
Waar hij langs komt wordt naar hem omgezien.
'Wat?' zegt iemand 'kent u Awater niet?
Ik meen, hij is accountant of zoiets.
Ik ken hem, maar ik ken hem niet intiem.
Sommigen zeggen, 's avonds leest hij Grieks,
maar anderen beweren het is Iers.' –
Er is intussen iets zeer vreemds geschied.
Een heer die zich op 't podium verhief

zegt dat hij Awater zijn plaats aanbiedt.
'Ik spreek' zegt hij 'uit naam van allen hier.
Wij hebben tussen ons een groot artiest.'
Awater, met gebaren naar 't servies,
wil zeggen dat hij van de eer afziet
en liever had dat men hem eten liet.
In de biljartzaal staakt men een serie.
Het wordt doodstil. Boven schaart men nieuwsgierig
zich langs de balustrade der verdieping.
Het schroefblad van de ventilator wiekt.
Dan staat Awater op en zingt zijn lied:
– Steeds troostte ze, steeds heeft zij als ik sliep
mij met haar liefelijke komst bezield,
de aanbedene; thans kwam ze en heeft vernield
de laatste steun die mijn verlies zich schiep.
Zij was, toen 'k haar ontwaren ging, in diep
met schrik vermengd verdriet teneergeknield;
ik hoorde dat zij mij geloof voorhield
maar zonder dat het hoop of vreugde opriep:
'Herinnert ge u die laatste avond niet'
sprak ze 'toen ik uw tranen heb ontzien
en zonder meer de wereld achterliet?
Ik kon, noch wilde ik, melden u sindsdien
hetgeen ik thans u te verstaan gebied:
niet hopen mij op aarde ooit weer te zien.'
Awater zwijgt. Hij verstijft tot graniet.
Men applaudisseert, werpt met serpentines.
Awater, als een pop, als een pop die

te zwaar is voor zijn eigen mechaniek,
waggelt de uitgang toe dwars door 't publiek.
Er wappert nog een smalle strook papier
hem langs de rug. Ik volg hem op de hielen.

Ik zorg – want het is stil en de straat nauw –
gelijke tred met Awater te houden.
Zo hoort hij niet dat iemand hem bijhoudt.
Mijn bezorgdheden worden menigvoud:
er ligt post thuis, ik heb aan de werkvrouw
nog niet gezegd dat ik op reis gaan zou,
mijn raam staat aan, er brandt vuur in de schouw,
ik heb niets bij me, wat doe ik überhaupt
op reis te gaan. – De vlieger aan zijn touw
tuimelt en stijgt: telkens slaat mijn benauwdheid
in vaster blijdschap om: wat zou 't, wat zou 't!
Zo voer ik, het hoofd diepgebogen houdend,
met mijzelf het beslissend onderhoud.
De straat wordt breder. Uit bomen druipt dauw.
Recht voor ons uit ligt het stationsgebouw.
Zou men hier middernacht een meeting houden?
't Is stampvol op het plein. Tussen flambouwen
staat op een ruw getimmerte van hout
in haar heilsuniform, een jonge vrouw.
Toeristen met rugzakken op de schouders,
kinderen, vrouwen, arbeiders, hun blauw
werkpak nog aan, staan onder de toeschouwers.
'Wij leven' zegt zij 'heel ons leven fout.'

Awater, die de pas heeft ingehouden,
kijkt naar mij om als kent hij mij vanouds.
Maar waar? in een tram? in een schouwburgpauze?
zo vraagt de blik waarmee hij mij beschouwt,
terwijl hij — want het waait — zijn hoed vasthoudt.
Wind, spelend met haar haar, legt langs de mouw
der heilssoldaat een losse knoop van goud.
'Liefde' zegt zij, 'wordt nooit vergeefs vertrouwd.'
Awater blijft, ik loop door, en zo gauw
of ik de trein zag die ik halen wou.

De stoker werpt steenkolen op het vuur.
De machinist staat leunend uit te turen.
Buiten de kap, boven de railsfiguren,
beginnen de signalen hun prelude.
De klok verspringt van minuut naar minuut.
Weer roept zij, de locomotief; voortdurend
roept zij, roepend dat het te lang reeds duurt.
Haar zuil van zuchten wordt een wolkenkluwen.
Maar denk niet, dat zij zich bekreunt om u,
de Oriënt Express; nog minder deelt ze uw jubel
als gij plaatsnamen ziet in een schriftuur
die de eerste klank is van het avontuur.
Zij kent in haar reisvaardigheid geen rücksicht.
Wat voor hoop gij ook koestert of wegduwt,
nogmaals, het deert haar niet; zelfs voor de illusie
een reisgenoot te hebben is ze immuun.
Dat gij, geheel alleen, u in haar luxe

beklemd voelt, 't raampje neerlaat, en zelfs nu
't perron nog afblikt; of dat gij het puurst
geluk smaakt dat voor het individu
is weggelegd: te weten, 'k werd bestuurd,
't is niet om niet geweest, ik was geen dupe, –
geprezen! – 't laat haar koud. Zij ziet azuur.
Van schakels is haar klinkende ceintuur.
Zij zingt, zij tilt een knie, door stoom omstuwd.
Zij vertrekt op het voorgeschreven uur.

Utrecht, 1934

Awater

TRANSLATED BY DAVID COLMER

'wanted: a travelling companion'

Be here with me, immortal timeless being
that moves upon the face of nascent waters.
You cannot but look kindly on this work,
it is as void and formless as the world.
Unlike the age now past, it has no wish
to see debris and sing of sunny weather,
for song is merely passion from a wound
and nothing whatsoever's been destroyed.
The cornerstone has only just been laid.
Each word renews the silence that it breaks.
What happens now will happen for the first.
Be praised! For Noah builds, but not an ark.
Jonah preaches, but not at Nineveh.

I've seen a man. He doesn't have a name.
Just give him all our first names rolled in one.
He is a father's son and born of woman.
Each morning by the rosy light of dawn,
he leaves his suburb, walking past my window.

When evening blues the sky, he comes back home.
At work his colleagues know him as Awater.
Behold this man who's clad in camel's hair
thread through a needle's eye. His meagre body
is fed on meals of honeycomb and locusts.
The meaning of his cries is lost to all.
It's wilderness where he lifts up his arms.
He has a monkish air, a soldier's look,
but no one says a prayer or blows a horn
when solemn books are opened at the office.
They sit at desks as if they're in a temple
and write in Arabic mixed with Italian.
Columns of enigmatic words rise up
in numbers fluttering down like flakes of ash.
Inside the silent room the summer's back.
A salty tang wafts from the steady clack
of metal hammers typing balderdash.
Read it, it doesn't say what it says. It says:
'Oh, Mother, you will never wear the fur
you counted every penny to afford,
and I won't come into your public ward
on my days off with flowers in my hand . . .
I'll take the roses to Churchyard Row instead.'
That's what it says. Awater's stony face
shows motionless how deeply he is moved.
What time is it? He rests his heavy head.
The phone is sleeping on a green baize bed.
The cups have been collected on a trolley.

The clock ticks – chimes – ticks and ticks until five
    thirty.
It chimes again and all the lamps go out.

Watering the flowers on my windowsill
this afternoon, I felt a firm resolve
to go and fetch Awater from his office.
I've been alone now since my brother's death.
When looking for a travelling companion,
one finds out first if one can get along.
That's why tonight I'll be Awater's shadow
and bide my time until I have his measure –
to maybe introduce myself tomorrow.
I've forged that plan. But here, before the steps,
I hesitate. Five-thirty sounds and time expands.
The street becomes a stream of passers-by.
Each patch of darkness slows to strike a light,
creating wandering smoke-drawn silhouettes.
Brother in heaven, be here with me as well.
Protect me. Keep me shadowy, unlit.
Preserve me as I am, unseen, unheard . . .
Suddenly Awater's there, blinking his eyes.
I watch him on the final flight of stairs.
No mortal soul, no town, no glow of dusk
exists for him. He hurriedly descends
the sandstone steps between the two brass snakes,
eyes fixed, it seems, on some remote horizon
where constant bolts of lightning charge the sky.

He rushes past so fast it seems as if
he's seen the place he hopes to find and heard
the thing he dreams about, and I feel pierced.
He doesn't slow, but hurries through the lobby
to hang his key up on a numbered hook.
He sees a brittle thistle standing there,
picks up his cane and, whistling, saunters off.
His hat is on, but I now bare my head:
Be here again with me, you who dwell at heights
as desolate and harsh as Calvary.

The road outside is paved with dark grey asphalt.
I notice that the echo that followed me through
the white-tiled hall falls silent at the door.
The town endows my feet with noiselessness.
A line of cars in caravan glides past;
I hear the sound of softly creaking leather.
Awater has already hurried on.
It seems he really does intend to travel.
I watch him stop at the department store
to contemplate a group of mannequins,
who – with binoculars and picnic rugs –
are clearly bivouacked upon the Nile,
as shown by palm trees, Sphinx and Bedouins.
Awater, I can tell what you are thinking
a few steps further down the street, where there's
a poster for a shipping line that shows
a desert Arab raising up one hand

to greet a ship that's come from distant lands,
and, further still, at the palatial bank
that lists the rates for foreign currencies.
We carry on together past the shop-fronts
until he shoots abruptly down a side-street.
A shop bell rings. He must have gone inside.
A notice on the door says, Cut and Shave.
The small salon is flanked by shelves and cupboards
and so awash with the overpowering reek
of toiletries that it seems smaller still.
Awater – I must admit I'm quite relieved
to see him, he'd almost given me the slip –
is sitting at a round ceramic sink
wrapped tightly in a cloak of starched white linen.
The barber does his job and I pretend
to be the next in line and take a seat.
I've never seen Awater closer by
than in this mirror; never has he appeared
so absolutely inaccessible.
Between the bottles, glittering and splintered,
he rises in the mirror like an iceberg
the scissors' shining bows go gliding past.
But spring comes soon, and with the mist still hanging
from a sudden passing shower, the barber's comb
now ploughs a furrow in his tousled hair.
Awater pays and leaves the barbershop.
I follow him without a second thought.

Chance takes a short cut to its destination.
Was it meant to be – Awater's ending up
in the bar I used to visit with my brother?
It was: he's even occupied our corner.
I sit down somewhere else. It's hardly full.
The barman knows me. He knows the way I feel.
He wipes my table for a second time
and dawdles with the white cloth in his hand.
'The times,' he mumbles finally, 'have changed.'
I know that he is thinking of my brother:
the way he used to breeze in with his dog
and his fedora tilted slightly back,
bringing a breath of life into the place.
The same grey sand is covering the floor,
the same grey dove is cooing in its cage.
Whoosh, says the wind, on, on! Enough's enough.
Who's that? I say, for want of something better,
and he, quite sure of whom I mean, replies,
'I've never seen him here before. He's new.'
Returning to the bar, he shuts the flap
and starts to rinse the glasses in the sink.
Awater looks for something in his pocket.
It is a book of plain Moroccan green.
It is a chess set when it's opened up.
A cool and distant look comes to his eye.
His fingers drum the table to embolden
the vision that goes whirling through his mind.
A single snowflake swirls through drops of blood.

He moves the men into their new position.
His untouched glass turns pale with condensation.
The cigarette that he's forgotten glows
and grows a stem that blossoms on the ceiling.
He sits aloof and perfectly alone.
He has a deeply moving inner force,
like that within a planet or a flower.
But now he drains his glass and shuts the book.
Gazing into space, he's somehow wistful.
He looks my way and I can't help but think
it's me he's calling when he calls the barman.
But no, he pays, and so do I, and soon
we're back out on the bustling streets again.

Bursts of electric light on the façade
keep writing and rewriting the restaurant name.
A doorman at the glass revolving door
is posted there to help a double queue
of people in and out. We go in too
and hear the sound of music as we enter.
Awater is no stranger here it seems.
Heads turn as he strolls in between the tables.
'What?' whispers someone. 'Don't you know Awater?
I think he's an accountant, some such thing.
I *do* know him, I just don't know him well.
Some say he spends his evenings reading Greek,
but others claim it's actually Irish Gaelic.'
Meanwhile something unusual has happened.

A man who'd climbed the steps up to the stage
has asked Awater if he'll take his place.
'I speak,' he says, 'for everybody here.
A great artiste is present in our midst.'
Awater gestures at the empty table
as if to say that he declines the honour;
he'd rather people left him to his dinner.
Silence descends. A billiard player stops
his game mid-break. Upstairs the eager guests
move forward to the balustrade and wait.
Above us all, the ceiling fan is turning.
Awater then stands up and sings his song.
– She always came to comfort me at night,
her presence breathing life into my sleep,
until at last my loved one came to sweep
aside the consolation of my plight.
I turned and saw her kneeling on my right,
bent low by fear and overwhelming grief.
I heard her sing the merits of belief,
but lost at once my hope and all delight.
'Have you forgotten our last night,' she sighed,
'when I allowed your tears to censor me
and slipped out of the world so silently?
Since then I could not speak for all I tried
to say what I must now state clear and plain:
You will not see my face on earth again.'
Awater now falls silent. He's turned to stone.
The people clap their hands and some throw streamers

until Awater, like a clockwork toy
too heavy for its failing mechanism,
goes tottering past the tables to the exit,
with a narrow strip of paper trailing
from one shoulder. I follow on his heels.

I do my best to match my steps to his
so he won't hear that he is being followed –
it's quiet out and streets round here are narrow.
A host of cares and worries spring to mind:
there's post at home, I haven't told the cleaner
that I am leaving on a trip, the window's
open, the coals are glowing on the grate,
I haven't got a thing with me, what do
I think I'm doing going travelling?
The kite falters, tumbles, then soars. Again
my fears veer up as joy: let it all go!
And so, with head hung low, I carry on
this crucial conversation with myself.
The street grows wider. Dewdrops drip from trees.
It seems we're heading for the railway station.
Is a meeting being held there at this hour?
The square is packed. Up on a wooden stage
four flaming torches flank a woman, young,
dressed in Salvation Army uniform.
Her audience includes some children, mothers,
tourists with heavy packs slung over shoulders
and labourers in dark-blue boiler suits.

'We live our lives all wrong,' she says and pauses.
Awater, who has slowed and stopped, turns back
and studies me as if he knows my face.
I see a look in his eyes that seems to ask,
Where from? A tram? A theatre intermission?
It's blowing hard. His hand is on his hat.
Wind, playing with her hair, lays down a loop
of gold on the Salvationist's black sleeve.
'No one,' she says, 'has ever loved in vain.'
Awater stays, I carry on and dash
as if I've seen the train I hope to catch.

The stoker shovels coal into the fire.
The engine driver leans out of his window.
Out past the roof, above the lacing lines,
the signals start to play departure's song.
The clock's long hand leaps forward on the minute.
She calls, the Orient Express, and calls anew,
she calls that it is taking much too long.
Her pillared sighs become a mass of cloud.
Don't think her lamentations are for you,
still less that she might share in your delight
at seeing place-names in an alphabet
that strikes the first notes in adventure's tune.
Her head of steam is totally single-minded.
Whatever hopes you have or push aside,
again, she doesn't care; she's even immune
to illusions of having a travelling companion.

Whether you sit alone in stifling comfort,
lower the window and scan the platform yet,
or whether you now taste the purest joy
a man can ever hope to reach: knowing,
it wasn't just a waste, there was a guide
who led me here, I'm not a fool – be praised! –
it leaves her cold. Her eyes are on the sky.
Her clanking girdle's forged from links of iron.
She sings, her knees inch up in clouds of steam.
She moves and leaves at the appointed time.

Utrecht, 1934

Awater

TRANSLATED BY JAMES S. HOLMES

Wanted:
a travelling companion

Be present here, spirit primordial
that hovers over waters of beginning.
Bend your benignant eye upon this work:
it is as void and formless as the earth.
Its aim is not, as in a previous age,
to see the rubble heaps and sing fair skies,
for song is but the passion of a fester,
never rubble, whatever else it was.
A first stone's barely lowered in its place.
Each word renews the silence it disturbs.
All that now happens happens the first time.
Be praised! For Noah builds, but now no ark,
and Jonah preaches, far from Nineveh.

I've seen a man. A man who has no name.
Give him all of our given names in one.
He is some woman's and some father's son.
As soon as the red sun is in the sky
he goes toward town. He passes underneath

my window. Dusk falls: he comes back again.
He's at an office, there he's called Awater.
Behold him. He is clad in camel's hair
strung through a needle's eye. His body's lean,
nourished on locusts and wild honeycomb.
What he calls no one's ever understood.
Where he gesticulates is wilderness.
There's something in him of the monk, the soldier,
but there's no praying, and no bugle blown,
when at the office books are opened up.
They sit at desks as if they're in a temple.
They mix Italian script with Arabic.
From figures tumbling down the page like ash
columns of Delphic language rise aloft.
It grows still, it grows warmer in the room.
Thin rattling metal wafts more and more salt.
Typewriters daydream stuff and nonsense. Read:
what it says is not what it says. It says:
'O Mother, you will never wear the furs
you scrimped and scavenged every penny for,
and on my days off now I do not go
with flowers to the hospital; I take
the roses out to Cemetery Lane . . .'
This it says, and Awater's countenance,
motionless and intent, shows his emotion.
What time is it? Awater's head grows heavy.
The telephone sleeps on the writing desk.
The teacups are collected and returned.

The clock tick-tocks, strikes, ticks till half-past five
strikes. In the room the green lamps are put out.

Today, while I was watering the plants
beside the window, it occurred to me
to meet Awater when he left his office.
I've had no travelling companion since
my brother died. When you seek out a friend
it's natural to want to find out first
if you can get along with one another.
Tonight, then, I'll pursue Awater's trail;
I'll watch to see which way the cat will jump,
as people say, and then if all goes well,
tomorrow I shall introduce myself.
So here I stand, beside the entryway.
I'm filled with qualms. A clock strikes half-past five.
Time has a stop. Wayfarers flood the streets.
In every shadow is a light ignited
that in its wandrings shapes contours in smoke.
Brother in heaven, too, be present here.
Protect me, let my shade reveal no light.
Hold me invisible, inaudible.
– All at once Awater. I see him at
a turning of the stair, blinking his eyes.
For him there is no place, no person, no
red evening sky. He hurries down along
the sandstone stairs past twisting snakes of bronze.
He seems to see a distance, a horizon,

where lightning flashes sempiternally.
It is as if he hears the thing he dreams of,
and sees the whereabouts he hopes to find,
the way he rushes by; I feel transfixed.
He strides across the vestibule in haste.
He hangs a key among the other keys.
There is a dried-out thistle on his coat;
he grasps his cane and saunters whistling forth.
He puts his hat on; I, though, bare my head:
Once more, be present, you who dwell on heights
as inhospitable as Calvary.

The streets are asphalted. I notice that
the echo that had kept me company
along the grey-tiled hall falls still outside.
The city lends a muteness to the foot.
Caravan-like, a line of cars glides by,
passing us with a gentle creak of leather.
Awater has already hurried on.
Yes, yes, it must be so: he wants to travel.
He's stopped before a clothing-shop display.
I see that he is gazing at a group
of manikins with plaids and telescopes –
camping along the lush shores of the Nile,
so pyramids and palm-trees indicate.
O Awater, I know what you are dreaming,
there farther on, before a shipping-line
poster of a Bedouin in the desert

hailing a ship that heaves in sight at sea,
and farther still, before a banking house
where rates for foreign currency are quoted.
Thus we proceed along the shop displays.
Then suddenly he's vanished down a side street.
A shopbell rings. He must have gone inside.
The sign reads: haircuts, shaves. The pungent smell
of every make and mark of toiletry
makes the small room with cupboards on each side
seem smaller still. Awater – I must say
I'm glad to see him, I had almost lost him –
is seated in a robe of clear-starched linen
before a basin of white porcelain.
The barber's at his work, and I sit down
off to one side, as if to wait my turn.
I've never seen Awater from so near
as in the mirror now; at the same time
he's never seemed so never-reachable.
Among the bottles, luminously broken,
he rises in the mirror like an iceberg
along which the smooth scissors brush their beak.
But spring arrives, a passing shower's mists
hover round about, then the barber's comb
ploughs a straight parting through the tangled hair.
Awater leaves the barbershop, and I
follow him down the street, mechanically.

Chance sometimes takes a bypath to its goal.
Must it needs be Awater had to choose
the same café I went to with my brother?
It must needs be, he even takes our corner.
I sit down somewhere else. There's room enough.
The waiter knows me. He knows what I'm feeling.
This is the second time he's cleaned my table.
He lingers for a while beside my chair
in silence, with the white cloth in his hand.
'The times,' he says, 'aren't what they used to be.'
I know he's thinking of my brother too,
how he would breeze in with his dog in leash,
his hat pushed back a little on his head,
and fill the whole room with his hue and cry.
The same sand still is lying on the floor,
the same dove cooing in its cage as then.
Whoo, said the wind, on, on. It's best this way.
'Who's that?' I say, because I must say something.
And, knowing whom I mean at once, he says,
'Someone that's never been in here before.'
With that he pulls the bar-gate shut behind him
and sets to rinsing glasses in the water.
– What is Awater hunting in his pockets?
It is a booklet in morocco green.
No, it's a chess game, now he's opened it.
Awater's eyes gaze, cool and reticent.
His hands that drum the table-top encourage
the vision that goes raging through his forehead.

A snowflake flutters amidst drops of blood.
He shifts the chessmen to a new arrangement.
His glass frosts over, still untouched, before him.
In the ashtray his cigarette creates
a hollyhock that blooms along the ceiling.
He sits there quite alone and undisturbed.
He has the thing a flower has, and a planet,
an inward impetus that transports far.
But now he drains his glass and shuts his book.
Sitting there gazing straight ahead, he's something
sad about him. He looks my way, and when
he calls the waiter I think he means me.
But no, he pays his check. I do the same,
and soon we're moving through the crowd again.

Electric lights that shoot along the front
write out the title of the restaurant
time after time, and there's a double file
of people moving in-out past the doorman
who serves the entry of revolving glass.
As we go in, there is the sound of music.
Awater is well known here, so it seems.
People look round at him as he goes past.
'What?' says somebody, 'don't you know Awater?
I think he's an accountant, some such thing.
I know him, but don't know him very well.
Some people say that he reads Greek at night,
though other people will contend it's Erse.'

   – But meanwhile something very strange has happened.
A man has risen on the podium
and says he yields his place to Awater.
'I speak for everybody here,' he says.
'We have a great artiste within our midst.'
Awater makes a gesture toward his plate,
trying to say that he declines the honour
and would prefer to be allowed to eat.
The billiard players interrupt a break.
It's stockstill. People curiously range
along the railing of the mezzanine.
The fanblade of the ventilator turns.
Awater rises then and sings his song:

> *She, the loved one, would come, wont to console me,*
> *wont to inspire me in my very sleep*
> *by her approach; now she has come and broken*
> *the last support that shored my loss's need.*
>
> *When I descried her figure she was kneeling*
> *in a deep sadness intermixed with fear;*
> *I heard her bid me not to cease believing,*
> *but without feeling either hope or cheer:*
>
> *'Do you remember that last night together,'*
> *she said, 'when I respected your hot tears*
> *and left the world behind, and all its worth?*

After that night I could not, would not tell you
the tiding I must now commend your ears:
nevermore hope to see me on this earth.'

Awater stops. He stiffens into stone.
The crowd applauds and tosses paper streamers.
Awater, like a doll, a doll that is
too heavy for its mechanism, staggers
across the crowded room and to the exit.
There's still one strip of paper fluttering
along his back. I follow at his heels.

I try to keep step with Awater's step,
for it is quiet and the street is narrow.
This way he won't hear someone's following.
My cares are manifold: there's post at home,
I haven't told the maid I'd be away,
my window's open, there's fire in the hearth,
I've nothing with me; and why, anyway,
should I go travelling? – Upon its string
the kite tosses and soars: each perturbation
shifts to more steadfast joy. What then, what then?
And with my head bowed down I carry on
the crucial conversation with myself.
The street grows wider. Dew drips from the trees.
The railway station looms up straight ahead.
Is there a midnight meeting being held?
It's jam-packed in the square. Amid torch flames

stands a young woman, a salvationist,
upon a platform rudely built of wood.
Tourists with rucksacks slung across their backs,
women, children, and workers with their blue
workclothes still on make up her audience.
'We live our lives all wrong,' she starts to say.
Awater, who has stopped, looks round at me
as if he thinks he'd met me long ago.
But where? a tram? the intermission of
a play? inquires the gaze he turns on me,
holding his hat, because the wind has risen.
Wind, playing with the soldieress's hair,
lays on her sleeve a loose-tied knot of gold.
'One never puts one's trust in love in vain,'
she says. Awater stays, I hurry on,
as if I'd seen the train I had to catch.

The fireman tosses coal upon the fire.
The engineer leans out and stares ahead.
Beyond the station roof, above the rail
patterns, the signals start their overture.
The clock's hands jump from minute on to minute.
The locomotive calls, time after time,
calls that it has been waiting far too long.
Its pile of sighs becomes a clew of clouds.
But do not think its fretting is for you,
this Orient Express; nor does it share
your joy at seeing placenames in a script

that is adventure's opening accord.
Its readiness to travel is relentless.
Whatever hopes you cherish or reject,
it does not care, it is immune to even
the fancy of a travelling companion.
That you, alone in all its luxury,
put down the window with a heavy heart
and cast one final glance along the platform;
or that you taste that sheerest human bliss:
to know that you were guided, it was not
without a reason, you have not been duped –
be praised – it does not care. It sees blue skies.
Its clanking girdle is of iron links.
It sings, it lifts a knee, enswathed by steam.
And it departs at the appointed time.

A Note by the Translator

JAMES S. HOLMES

The Dutch text of *Awater* is technically something of a *tour de force*. Nijhoff, casting back to the vowel rhymes of the *Song of Roland* to give form to his poem, confined himself to no more than eight vowel sounds for his rhyme scheme, making each line rhyme assonantally with every other line in the same section. Short of writing a new poem, I could see no way to retain this element in the translation.

A second formal element borrowed from the *Song of Roland* is Nijhoff's strong emphasis on the end-stopped line: three-fourths of the lines in *Awater* conclude with a punctuation mark of some kind, and more than half of them have a full stop. The result is a stress on the isolated individual line that is unequalled even in neo-classical English verse. I have tried to keep as many of these end-stopped lines as I could, the more willingly because in the absence of Nijhoff's rhyme scheme they would help me to avoid the pitfall of easy traditionalism characteristic of much enjambed blank verse.

Awater

TRANSLATED BY DAAN VAN DER VAT

'Wanted, a travelling companion.'

Primordial Ghost, Spirit of Genesis,
Haunting the waters of earth's infancy,
Abide with me and bend Thy gracious eyes
Upon this work, which out of chaos rising
Appears as void and formless as the earth.
It does not, like a former age of song,
Glorify ruins, sing of sun or skies.
For singing is but festering utterance,
And naugh that ever was has yet decayed.
Foundation stones have hardly found their beds,
All words renew the silence they disturbed,
And naught that happens ever was before.
Praised be the Lord! For Noah wields his axe,
Though not intent upon another ark,
And Jonah preaches, far from Nineveh.

I saw a man, a man that bears no name,
Let our joint Christian names encompass him,

Some father's son born from some mother's womb.
When rosy dawn incarnadines the East,
He passes by my window towards the town
Not to return until the evening dusk.
He is a clerk. Awater he is called
By fellow-clerks. Behold him as he goes.
The hair of camels, threaded through eyes
Of needles, clothes his body. He is lean,
Because he feeds on locusts and wild honey.
No man has grasped the meaning of his call,
And only deserts form his audience:
Mixture of monk and soldier, unproclaimed.
For when the books are opened in the office,
No prayers are said. There are no trumpets blown.
How like a priest he thrones behind his desk
Mixing Arabian with Italian script.
Sibylline columns rise oracular
Above the fallen dust of ashen cyphers.
The silence grows. The room gets warm and warmer.
The substance of metallic rattling fades.
Typewriters murmuring unmeaning prattle
Have gone insane. Symbols have lost their sense.
'Mother of mine,' they say, 'when shall I ever
See you go clad in furs? Has now perhaps
My bunch of roses reached the hospital?'
Awater's face is carefully clean-shaven.
What is the time? The hours weigh down his head.
The telephone has long since gone to sleep.

An office-girl collects the empty tea-cups.
The green lamps are extinguished on the desks.

Watering the flowers on the window-sill
This morning I made up my mind to meet
Awater at his office. (I have been
A lonely traveller since my brother's death.)
There's nothing strange, when you desire a friend,
In wanting to discover if your choice
Will prove congenial. That is why tonight
You see me following in Awater's tracks.
I play a waiting game as one might say.
For who can tell the blessings of to-morrow?
So here I wait outside the office entrance
And guard the steps. Why should I feel self-conscious?
A clock strikes half past five. Time grows eternal.
Pedestrians flock past me through the street.
Tremulous lights, which blossom in dark corners,
Trace fleeting images in erring smoke.
Descend from heaven, brother, unto me,
Protect my shade from visibility
And let my going be unseen, unheard.
Awater suddenly appears. I watch
Him cross a landing, see him blink his eyes.
Humanity, nor town, nor evening glow
Exist for him. He rushes down the stairs,
Down sandstone steps, midst serpents of cold brass.
He looks as though his eyes beheld horizons

Where ceaseless lightning glorifies the skies.
As though he listened to his inmost dreams
And saw the spot where his own quest will end,
He rushes past. I feel my soul transfixed
As hurriedly he passes through the hall
And leaves his key upon the porter's desk.
A desiccated thistle strikes his eye.
He grasp his ash-plant, whistling as he goes,
And dons his hat. But I take off my hat.
Once more, descend, inhabitant of heights
As inaccessible as Calvary.

The streets are asphalt-paved. The echoes which
My steps woke in the tiled hall lag behind.
The tumult of the town has hushed my feet.
A murmurous complaint of creaking leather
Accompanies a file of passing cars.
Awater is already well ahead.
It must be true that he will go abroad.
For outside a men's shop I see him pause
To look upon a group of dummies which,
Judging by palm-trees and a pyramid,
Are camped upon the green banks of the Nile
With topees, travelling-rugs and cameras.
Oh Awater, somebody shares your dreams,
When further down the street you pause a while
Before the poster of a shipping-firm
On which a Bedouin in the desert greets

A ship appearing on a distant sea,
And when still further on, outside a bank,
You scan the rates of foreign currencies.
Thus we proceed along the lighted shops.
All of a sudden he takes to a side-street.
A doorbell rings. He must have entered here.
The window says: Shaving and Haircutting.
The little room with cupboards all around
Seems smaller still, for it is occupied
By an immense variety of scents.
Awater – whom I had almost lost and whom
I'm therefore very pleased to see again –
Is seated stiffly robed in starched attire
Before a basin of white porcelain.
The barber starts his work and I sit down,
Aside, alone, as if to bide my turn.
I've never seen Awater from so near
As I do now, eyeing him in the glass.
Nor has he ever seemed so far away.
Among the bottles, luminously broken,
He towers in the mirror like an iceberg
On which the tapering scissors form a beak.
But spring arrives. A vernal shower descends
Leaving a haze which slowly fades away,
While through the restless hair the barber's comb
Ploughs a straight furrow. Awater stands up
And takes his leave. I follow him outside.

Is there a God who shapes our destinies,
That Awater should choose the very inn
Where once I and my brother used to go?
Thus it was written. Thus it had to be.
He even occupies our corner seat.
I choose another seat. There's room galore.
The waiter knows me, knows my feelings too.
This is the second time he cleans my table.
He stands a long time silent by my chair
With his white napkin dangling from his hand.
At last he almost whispers: 'Times have changed.'
I know his memory has conjured up
The image of my brother breezing in,
Holding his dog in leash, his hat awry
Pushed back upon his head. He used to fill
The inn with noise. The selfsame sand is there
Tracing its figures on the floor and still
The selfsame turtle-dove coos in its cage.
The wind cried: 'Hie, pass on!' It had to be.
'Who's he?' I ask, wanting to say something.
I need not tell the waiter whom I mean.
'It is the first time I have seen him here.'
With this the waiter moves behind the bar,
He turns to close the wooden counter-flap
And starts to rinse the glasses in the sink.
My quarry lays an object on the table
Which, though resembling a green pocket-book,
Appears to be a chess-board when unfolded.

His pensive eye becomes almost forbidding.
His fingers drumming on the table-top
Embolden the conceit behind his brow.
– A snowflake gently falls midst drops of blood –
On the small board the game is rearranged.
Untouched, the glass before him becomes blurred.
His cigarette becomes a glowing root
From which a holly-hock rising aloft
Flowers along the ceiling of the inn.
He sits there quite alone and undisturbed.
His is the inner urge of flowers and planets
Which stirs the heart to dream and ecstasy.
He drains his glass and pots the book away.
His pensive face assumes a wistful look.
He looks my way and calls. Does he mean me?
He only wants to pay. I follow suit
And through the crowded streets he leads the way.

Electric lights which play on the façade
Write and re-write incessantly the name
Of the café. People in double queues
Enter and leave past the commissionaire
Who stands on guard near the revolving doors.
Soft music greets our entrance. Awater
Seem to be popular, for where he goes
People look up, follow him with their eyes.
'Surely, you know him,' says a customer,
'He's an accountant, something of the sort.

We are acquainted, but no more than that.
Some people say that he reads Greek at night,
Though I have heard it said he studies Erse.'
Meanwhile a strange event is taking place.
A gentleman who stands upon the stage
Enquires whether Awater will oblige.
'I know,' he says, 'that all of you agree
We have an artist in our company.'
My quarry, pointing at his dinner-plate,
Desires to make it clear that he declines
The honour and would rather start his meal.
A billiard-player interrupts his break.
Dead silence reigns. Along the balconies
Curious spectators stare down on the stage.
A ventilator whimpers on the wall.
Awater rises and begins his song:

'Though you were gone, aye, gone beyond recall,
O love, my love, you hallowed every night
With your dear presence and the sheer delight
Of your bright image on the night's dark wall.

And I thanked God He had not taken all,
Though you had left the world of day and light,
– A man may live because he dreams at night –
I thought naught worse could evermore befall.

Until last night, when kneeling by my side
And bidding me not to lose faith you cried:
"Now be prepared to go your way alone!"

What have I done and how can I atone?
How shall I bear the burden of my pain,
If even at night I bide my love in vain?'

Silence ensues, followed by loud applause.
While gaudy streamers slither round his head,
Awater stands as though he were of stone.
Then like a doll in danger of collapse
Under the burden of its mechanism
He staggers past the tables to the door,
A paper ribbon fluttering forlorn
Along his back. I follow on his heels.

The street is silent and not very wide.
So I take care to walk in step with him
Lest he should hear that someone walks behind.
Many anxieties beset my mind.
Letters need answ'ring. I must tell the maid
That I am leaving. I must shut the window.
And in my room I left the fire alight.
I have no luggage. And what after all
Moves me to go abroad? The wayward kite,
Straining upon its string, comes tumbling down
Then to shoot upwards. Thus repeatedly

My perturbation turns to purer joy.
Why be concerned? Thus, with my head bowed down
I and my inner self make up my mind.
The pavement widens. From the trees drips dew.
The railway station looms up straight ahead.
Is there a midnight meeting in the square?
The place is crowded. Amidst smoking torches
On a rough structure of unpainted wood
Stands a young woman, a salvationist.
Tourists with rucksacks slung across their backs,
Labourers wearing dark-blue boilersuits,
Women and children form her audience.
'My dears,' she says, 'why don't we change our lives?'
Awater, who has joined the crowd, looks back
As if he thought he'd seen my face before.
'But where?' he seems to wonder. 'In a tram?
Or in the interval during a play?'
A strong wind blows, which makes him grasp his hat.
The same wind playing with the woman's hair
Flings round her sleeve a noose of clinging gold.
'No one,' she says, 'has ever loved in vain.'
Awater stays. I hurry on as if
I'd seen a train which I must run to catch.

The fireman shovels coal on to the fire.
Leaning aside the driver scans the night.
Beyond the platform, o'er the gleaming rails,
The semaphores intone their overture.

Slowly the clock devours the passing time.
Again the engine whistles and again,
Impatient to be off and on her way.
Her rhythmic sighs become a moaning cloud.
But if she frets, the Orient Express,
It is not you she is concerned about.
Nor does she share your bliss when you exult
Looking at place-names painted in a script
In which adventure has enshrined its soul.
Her readiness to travel does not brook
That your concern should speed her on her way.
Whatever be your hopes or your despair,
She does not care. If you delude your mind
With the fond hope that you have found at last
Another traveller to share your quest,
She stays unmoved. Why should she care that you,
Alone and by her luxury oppressed,
Open the window once again to look
Along the platform, or that you enjoy
The purest happiness that man can know:
The knowledge that you've not been victimized,
That destiny has mapped your pilgrimage,
And that you have not followed it in vain?
She does not care. She dreams of azure skies.
Rattling her girdle wrought of iron links
She chants, she bends a knee in clouds of steam
To leave at last at the appointed hour.

Awater in English

DAAN VAN DER VAT

In the Easter holidays of the year 1939, I was dining with
Nijhoff in a Nijmegen restaurant when he suddenly
remarked that he deeply regretted how severely his
readership was limited by the narrow confines of the
Dutch-speaking world. I found the passion with which
he spoke very moving and ventured to suggest that it
might be possible to find someone who could translate at
least some of his poems into English. He returned
continually to the subject throughout the rest of the meal
until finally, in desperation, I promised that I would
return home and not rest until I had translated *Awater*
into English.

I had special reasons for choosing *Awater*. With the
exception of Nijhoff's later work 'Uur U',* I knew of
no more haunting poem in our language. For me, there
is something almost frightening about *Awater*; it is some-
thing of a crystallized nightmare. I found the poem so
oppressive that I felt an aversion to the very thought of
giving up all my distance to it by setting to work on a
translation. I completed the first version in three days,
during which time I really was in an almost nightmare
state. Fourteen years later my wife still remembers me
pacing the house in wordless obsession, mumbling to
myself. I immediately sent that first version, with which
I was far from satisfied, to Nijhoff, and received the
following letter in reply. As is clear from his letter, Nijhoff

* 'Zero Hour' [DC]

was writing about a version that differed considerably from the one published here.

Zeist, 17 April, 1939
Kersbergenlaan 7 c.

Dear friend,

I am delighted, first by the conscientiousness with which you have immediately sent the promised speech and copies, and second by 'Bywater' [*This was the name that replaced 'Awater' in my original version. – D.v.d.V.*]. Really, this is an achievement. Again, I am delighted, and, if further encouragement from these quarters is required, let it be this: Awater rediscovers himself in Bywater as in a reflection that has stepped out of the frame and taken on an independent existence. This translation has the significance of an encounter. For me personally, it is like rediscovering a beloved figure. *Excusez moi, je ne suis qu'un poète.*

As far as the language is concerned, if your wife has no objections [*this refers to my wife's English nationality. – D.v.d.V.*], I have none either. Below are a few comments (not criticisms) that may be of some help:

Line

3.   *Tender looks . . . open eyes.*
4.   are 'wild' and 'hollow' the terms from Genesis?
10. *and each word had renewed the unbroken silence*
13. *though what he builds is no ark as before.*
14. yours is better than the Dutch!
18. *no sooner had the red sun dyed the east.*
19. *not to return until the blue eve's dusk?*
     The question mark applies to 'eve's'. Can we

make it: 'until blue evening dusk', i.e. without the 'the'? Then also in 18: instead of 'the red sun' – 'red sunrise'.

37. In your version this line is one foot too short. I suggest the following in combination with 38 for your consideration:

Type-writers murmur silly pratter. Symbols
Have lost their sense. You need but read: it's nonsense.

44. 'writing-desk' is not good because 47 also ends with 'desks'. I suggest something like: *the telephone sleeps between ink and pad.*

45. The word 'tea' must be included. 'An office girl' is excellent! Can we have: 'empty teacups' or 'teacups emptied' or something like that.

I beseech you, persevere with your work, and preferably as quickly as possible. Please!

I was very glad of the opportunity to see you again in Nijmegen and meet your wife.

> With fond regards,
> Yours,
> Nijhoff

P.S. I already know the spontaneous lines

– *Watering the flowers on the window-sill to-day*
– *whatever be your hopes or your despair*
– *'No one,' she says 'has ever loved in vain.'*

off by heart. In case you don't, I have copied them out for you above.

I kept working towards the completion of the definitive version and soon after sent Nijhoff a 'provisional' definitive translation, which I later continued to polish. I received the following letter.

Zeist, 25 April 1939
Kersbergenlaan 7c.

Dear friend,

My heartfelt thanks for the 'gift', as you put it, of the completed 'Bywater'. I am *very* happy with it, I admire your achievement. I'm sure you will agree with me that in art only the impossible is of value: well then, this translation, which I had considered impossible, has that value for me – Of course, I aim for publication. Why not? Shall we contact T. S. Eliot and ask his advice about a magazine or a chapbook?

Your suggestion of appointing Harting as a sympathetic jury is excellent. I would like very much to go through the text line by line with you and him, in a month's time, of course, after you have had a chance to recover from and rest after the enormous effort you must have put into it. Because you have done more than 'adequately fulfil your task'. And it is for this 'more' that I am most thankful.

I will see you next month in Amsterdam, then. Let me say once again how grateful I am.

Regards to your wife and fond greetings,

Yours,
Nijhoff

As I wished to further polish the translation, Nijhoff returned 'Bywater', as it was still called, three days later. He enclosed a short note.

Zeist, 28 April 1939
Kersbergenlaan 7c.

Dear friend,

Enclosed, please find 'Bywater'.

Just read your excellent piece on T. S. Eliot. In it you quote Mallarmé, his illusion of writing entirely without a *voix d'auteur*. Very appropriate. I will keep to that. I believe that you are underestimating 'The Journey of the Magi' and 'Marina' in particular. For me they are, with 'The Waste Land', *the* masterpieces. 'Marina' is from Shakespeare's *Pericles*. It is E.'s most tender poem, the start of re-blossoming. 'The Magi' form the breakthrough after his 'Ash Wednesday' period. After 'Marina', however, the fasting has now recommenced in the form of a wintry dogma.

At any rate, I enjoyed your piece.

Regards to your wife and fond greetings,

Yours,
Nijhoff

Soon after I received the following letter.

Zeist, 10 July 1939
Kersbergenlaan 7c

Dear and neglected friend,

This afternoon your postcard arrived, reminding me of my prolonged failure to make an appointment for an evening together (with Harting) in Amsterdam.

Please forgive me. I have been feeling rotten for a long time, since being discharged from service. The old depressions. Work that has gone wrong. You know the kind of thing. My peculiarity is that I then choose to keep a low profile.

On 19 July I won't be in Utrecht. On 15 July I am going to Walcheren, where I will be staying until 15 September. Address: Biggekerke, Zeeland. But on 14 July, this Friday, I will be in Amsterdam between 3 and 6. In the evening I have to go to Jan Engelsman's outdoor play. Will you happen to be in Amsterdam on Friday afternoon? If so, I will bring 'Bywater' with me. Don't you have a copy of it? No, you request it so emphatically I will enclose it now.

How are things going? I am very sorry that I won't be able to see you in Utrecht. 'Bywater' enclosed, I am very sorry to see it leave my room. I would give anything to be able to talk to you about it one quiet evening. Written in haste. Regards to your wife and fond greetings,

> Yours,
> Nijhoff

Nijhoff was right. I did have a copy of 'Bywater', but was unwilling to leave a copy of the translation in his possession while I was still so dissatisfied with it.

The next letter on this subject arrived a good two years later, in wartime.

> Utrecht, 4 October 1941

Dear Van der Vat,

Given that I was recently obliged to leave my rooms at the Janskerhof, and the difficulty of finding something suitable here, I am currently staying with friends and my postal address is as above: P. O. Box 126, Utrecht.

I am curious about 'Bywater'. Last winter I gave a lecture in Alkmaar and afterwards spent the entire evening trying to find you (in the Corfstraat, I believe). I went from house to house knocking on doors, but no luck. I notice now that you have moved.

Best wishes,
Yours,
Nijhoff

Nijhoff was now finally in possession of what he considered the definitive, final version of the English translation. Despite this, I continued to work on the translation during the war years. When, in 1944, I believed that I had come close to an acceptable final form, I wrote to Nijhoff asking him to return his, now superseded, copy to me. All this time, Nijhoff had continued to resist my use of the name Bywater for Awater, which, in an English pronunciation, sounded unpleasant to me.

The Hague, 11-5-'44
Kleine Kazernestraat 1a

Dear Van der Vat,

Thank you for your letter. I shall launch an investigation into the location of my copy of your translation as quickly as possible. The problem is, after being forced to move twice, I have lost many of my possessions, especially books and papers, because of the inadequate means of transportation available. Of course, I am most curious about the changes you have made. Something that still strikes me as strange is the name Bywater.

What made you decide to use it? There is a chance of my being in Alkmaar on Whit Monday. Will you be there then?

Fond greetings and my regards to your wife,

Yours,
Nijhoff.

In that same year of the war, I received a letter from Nijhoff informing me that there was talk of publishing the translation together with the Dutch original in the 'Volière' series. For reasons unknown to me, this publication did not, however, proceed.

The Hague, 25-8-44
Kleine Kazernestraat 1a

Dear Van der Vat,

I received a letter from Groningen from Mr Mooy (Marja) informing me that he intends to publish your translation of 'Awater' together with the original in the 'Volière' series. A nice idea and I very much hope that this publication will be of some gratification to you and partly reward the great effort and inestimable dedication you have put into and brought to this work.

Is there anything left that we need to discuss? Would you like to go through the whole poem together before dispatching the manuscript? As you are unwilling to come to The Hague, I could come to Alkmaar for an afternoon. [*For obvious reasons, I was somewhat reluctant to go to The Hague, as the circumstances of the time had forced me to go into hiding on a farm. D.v.d.V.*] We could then work from two to five. If you

can let me know which afternoons are most conve-
nient for you (i.e. Wednesday afternoons), I will decide
the week. One subject of discussion will definitely be
the title. I have never been able to reconcile myself to
'Bywater' – in which I hear something like 'a side
canal'. And if 'Awater' and 'Bywater' were now to be
printed alongside each other it would give a strange
impression. Is Arwater a possibility? Or Aywater?
Please give this some thought . . .

If you regularly visit Amsterdam, we could also
arrange an appointment there. After so many years, I
hope that our meeting will not fail as disastrously as on
the Whit Monday when I was in Alkmaar and desper-
ately walked up and down the Westerweg in the
scorching heat, not knowing your house number
because I had left your letter at home! I knocked on
the doors of a number of houses, but no one knew
where you lived!

Fond regards,

Yours,
Nijhoff

Our attempts to meet seemed cursed and the bad luck
continued until Nijhoff's death. In October of that same
year, I received this note:

The Hague, 15-9-44

Dear Van der Vat,

What do we do now? You realize that I couldn't face
the trip on Thursday 7 September. On the Tuesday
before it had taken me some 20 hours to get back to

The Hague from Utrecht.* There was congestion on the Thursday too.

It seems to me that we are better off corresponding. You know that my primary point of discussion is the name Awater. Make a proposal in that regard. I have difficulties with Bywater.

Very fond regards,
Yours,
N.

Unlike me, Nijhoff was unfamiliar with the name Bywater as an English surname, but an English pronunciation of Awater continued to sound unpleasant to my ears. Despite this I gave in to the pressure from Nijhoff and began using the name Awater in the translation as well. In October 1945 I moved to London. Repeated attempts on both sides to arrange a meeting during my brief visits to Holland failed without exception. Nijhoff had asked me to attempt to publish the translation in England. I remained, however, dissatisfied and continued to make small changes until the spring of 1949, when I was visited in London by Miron Grindea, editor of the international literary and cultural magazine *Adam: International Review*. He informed me that he was planning to dedicate the forthcoming July issue of his magazine entirely to the Netherlands and asked me if I could provide him with a translation of a prominent Dutch

---

* This was the day known in the Netherlands as Dolle Dinsdag, 'Mad Tuesday', when false rumours of an imminent Allied advance set off a panic amongst Germans and Dutch collaborators. There were chaotic scenes as many of them attempted to flee the country. [DC]

poem. I gave him *Awater* and informed Nijhoff immediately.

The Hague, 28 June, 1949
Kleine Kazernestraat 1

Dear Van der Vat,

I found your letter dated 13/6 yesterday after returning from a three-week trip to France. You realize that I am very gratified to receive news that our mutual 'Awater' is finally going to be published and I am very glad to give my permission. I would be pleased to receive a few copies and I expect that Dutch booksellers (e.g. Nijhoff in The Hague and Broese in Utrecht) would be glad to take a few copies as well. If it is necessary for me to stimulate R., just let me know.

I envy your living in England. Before we could imagine that we were living here, in our country, as if on a ship; now we live in a lifeboat. While faced with the greatest of problems here and overseas, we are more narrow-minded than ever. My current address is above. Keep in touch and accept my fond regards.

Yours,
Nijhoff

P.S. Have you seen the book with Barnouw's translations?

I never saw Nijhoff again, which I regret bitterly. But I am glad to have once been able to do a favour for such a good friend and such a great poet.

Translated by David Colmer

Retranslating *Awater*

DAVID COLMER

There can be many reasons for commissioning a retranslation of a literary work, but the perfection of a previous translation is seldom one of them. A translator could accept the job blind, and have many reasons for doing so, but I suspect that, like me, most translators would start by casting an eye over the previous translation or translations to see whether they agreed that a retranslation was necessary or desirable, identifying shortcomings in approach or execution, and deciding if and how the existing translations could be improved upon. More than just an implicit criticism of the work of one's predecessors, accepting the commission to retranslate becomes a reckless declaration of confidence in one's ability to do better.

When pondering whether to accept the job of translating Martinus Nijhoff's *Awater*, I was aware of two English translations: one by James S. Holmes and one by Daan van der Vat. The early translation by the Dutch poet, author and journalist, Van der Vat, is most interesting in its context: it was produced in consultation with Nijhoff himself and has been published together with the letters the poet wrote to Van der Vat about the translation. This version was something of a labour of love: Van der Vat started it shortly before World War II as a favour to an admired friend and polished it over a tumultuous decade before finally releasing it for publication.

In his translation Van der Vat seems to aim for a general tone that approaches the richness of the original. This is clear from the flowing assonance and alliteration of lines like:

> *Abide with me and bend Thy gracious eyes*
> *Upon this work, which out of chaos rising*
> *Appears as void and formless as the earth.*

If we exclude Van der Vat's initial plan of using a different name for the protagonist, there is nothing in the correspondence to suggest that either his interpretation or approach met with anything but approval from Nijhoff, who repeatedly expressed his gratitude and appreciation, describing the translation as an achievement – the attainment of something he had thought impossible.

Unfortunately, this achievement is most impressive in context. Van der Vat was obviously handicapped by translating into a foreign language and his Dutch-speaking background both increases and diminishes his accomplishment: it makes it a more remarkable feat, but also explains weaknesses in the translation that reduce its effectiveness as a poem in its own right and make it less useful as a gateway to the original. There is a recurring clumsiness, sometimes in word choice, sometimes in phrasing, that is visible in lines like:

> *The substance of metallic rattling fades.*
> *Typewriters murmuring unmeaning prattle*
> *Have gone insane. Symbols have lost their sense.*

but also between the lines, in the transition from one to the next, as if the translator is overstretched and sometimes needs to catch his breath before carrying on. Continuing the quote and comparing it to the Dutch alerts us to another point of concern:

> *'Mother of mine,' they say, 'when shall I ever*
> *See you go clad in furs? Has now perhaps*
> *My bunch of roses reached the hospital?'*

These three lines compare to five in the original version we know today. A look at Holmes shows the differences:

> *'O Mother, you will never wear the furs*
> *you scrimped and scavenged every penny for,*
> *and on my days off now I do not go*
> *with flowers to the hospital; I take*
> *the roses out to Cemetery Lane . . .'*

Thriftiness, the actual purchase of the coat and the death of Awater's mother – all are missing from Van der Vat's translation. Knowing that Van der Vat was extremely conscientious and had no difficulty understanding his native Dutch, these 'liberties' seem mysterious until we realize that the explanation is the obvious one, the one people so often overlook in their haste to blame a translator: it's the original that has changed! Van de Vat's *Awater* is a translation of an earlier version, a record of what was then a work in progress. It seems likely that the changes Nijhoff had made in the subsequent editions were one of the points he hoped to discuss in the meetings he tried to arrange with Van der Vat, meetings that were invariably thwarted by the chaos and dangers of the German occupation. In a sense, Van der Vat's translation was outdated even when first published sixty years ago.

Another important point that isn't mentioned in the correspondence between Nijhoff and Van der Vat is that, despite retaining the iambic pentameter and the rhyming sonnet (which the character Awater sings in the sixth section), Van der Vat does not try to reproduce the assonant rhyming structure that is the poem's most striking formal element. Had Van der Vat and Nijhoff discussed this in their initial conversation, rejected it as impossible to achieve in English, and moved on without further comment? It is, after all, scarcely conceivable that they could have simply ignored the whole issue. Whatever Nijhoff's and Van der Vat's reasoning, Holmes made the same choice around twenty years later, explaining in his rather cursory translator's note that: 'Short of writing a new poem, I could see no way to retain this element in the translation.'

Obviously a new translation that trumped both predecessors by fully retaining both content and form would need no further justification; however, I too, after some experimentation, concluded that the poem's rhyming scheme, in which all of the lines within a section end with the stress on the same vowel sound, was beyond me – at least without subjecting the English language to significant abuse, by which I mean archaism, inverted word order, strained pronunciation and other unnatural practices.

I don't discount the possibility of a more skilled translator being able to pull it off, but the difficulty is immense and should not be underestimated: the longest section is made up of 47 lines *with* the fully rhyming sonnet mentioned above *embedded* in the assonantal scheme. Getting the vowels to rhyme is one thing, getting them to rhyme while retaining meaning, metre and beauty of expression is another.

As an aside, it's worth noting that even if a translator were able to reproduce this rhyming scheme, they still wouldn't achieve the full effect of the original because the regularity of Dutch spelling means that the different sections of the poem work visually as well as audibly.

One glance at the page is enough for the reader to see whether they are reading the *aa* section, the *uu* section or the *oe* section. Given the infamous vagaries of our spelling, this feature would be impossible to achieve in English. Curiously enough, thinking about words in terms of their vowel sounds is so normal in Dutch that it can be seen on any traditional primer. The dipthong *eu*, for instance: illustrated by the first name *Teun* and a picture of an old man with a beard and a hat.

Although both translators reproduce the metre and not the assonant rhyme, Holmes and Van der Vat's translations are still worlds apart. Where Van der Vat seems to strive for some kind of equivalence to Nijhoff's poetic tone, Holmes plays it straight, with a low-key, fairly prosaic tone. His iambic clock ticks away through a faithful, close rendition of the Dutch, which, at its best, achieves the lucidity of the passage quoted above. Despite occasional peculiarities in word choice and interpretation ('for song is but the passion of a fester') his translation is more successful than Van der Vat's, but also less ambitious. It is almost as if, having decided to abandon end assonance as a structural feature, Holmes has gone on to deliberately avoid any kind of assonance, alliteration or internal rhyme. To my mind this falls unnecessarily short. It is important to realize that there are many more sound echoes present in the original – within individual lines and from line to line: assonance, alliteration and full rhyme – and that the assonantal end rhyme, while identifying the long sections, also dovetails with these other effects to create the rich sound and dense, almost incantatory feel of the poem throughout, even within much smaller units. Wouldn't it be truer to the original to try to maintain assonance as a characteristic element in the poem's music, despite being forced to abandon it as a regular structural element? Or does consistency demand that it be banished altogether? My natural inclination was to attempt to retain it in some way, trying to produce a translation that at least *suggested* the sound of Nijhoff's *Awater*, if only in desultory bursts.

This then was my justification for accepting the job and starting work on a new translation: I *aimed* to do more than Holmes and felt that I *could* do better than Van der Vat. Obviously the results are not for me to judge.

It is, however, worth mentioning that, from a twenty-first century perspective, one interesting criterion for judging a translation of Nijhoff's *Awater* is quotability. In the Netherlands the poem is extremely well known, highly influential and quoted to the point of excess. Phrases like 'er staat niet wat er staat' from the line 'Lees maar, er staat niet wat er staat. Er staat:' have taken on a life of their own and are referred to frequently in Dutch poetics and poetry reviews. (In my translation: 'Read it: it doesn't say what it says. It says:') Although I am under no illusion that the English translation will ever acquire a similar status, it would be nice if the translations of these classic one-liners reflected the aphoristic and enigmatic qualities of the original, so that it becomes possible for English readers to at least begin to understand why the poem continues to mean so much to Dutch poets and readers alike.

Having studied both the Holmes and Van der Vat translations before starting work, it's difficult to say just how much they influenced my own translation. Although the final versions show very little overlap, I did refer to both of them now and then to see how they had resolved questions of interpretation, and it's quite likely that their solutions helped to point me in particular directions. I also consulted Ard Posthuma's German translation when trying to resolve particularly thistly issues. I am grateful to Thomas Möhlmann and Benno Barnard for helping me to come closer to understanding the original, and to Sam Garrett and, again, Benno Barnard for reading a draft of the translation, offering criticism and making suggestions.

Amsterdam, January 2009

Poetry in a Period of Crisis

MARTINUS NIJHOFF

Martinus Nijhoff (1894–1953) completed his long poem Awater *in 1934. The next year he gave a talk at Enschede Folk University which affords a clearer insight than any critic could provide into his poetic aims and aspirations during those years of economic and intellectual crisis. The text of the talk was not published during the poet's lifetime; the following passages, those most closely having to do with the genesis of* Awater, *are from a draft of the talk found among his papers after his death.*

I started talking to the waiter when he came to my table to settle up. How was business doing? 'Poorly, sir,' said the waiter, 'we can certainly tell there's a crisis.' Our talk threatened to take on a less than cheerful note. I paid and set off for home.

The waiter's word 'crisis' nagged at me. During the boom years poetry may possibly have fallen short, to the extent that it had brought more self-glorification than self-exploration – though none of the great poets could be found guilty of anything like that. But what of poetry in a period of crisis? What interest could poetry demand at a time when the production of goods is no longer profitable? The street lights, a tram rattling by, a policeman standing at his post were clear proofs that the world was going on, that the producing agencies were still providing light, power, and energy, that the world of man had arrived at a kind of blind method, and the various parts went on rotating like the stars in a constellation. Whatever revolution the world's history may hold in

79

store, it will have to take over this order of trains, steamships, aeroplanes, factories, strict discipline. Man has built a technological structure across the world, and this structure functions as perfectly as the seasons, as day and night, as birth and death in nature. The tram is a star, the policeman is a star, even though they are stars that are moved along their courses by a propulsive force created by men, multitudes of men, generations of men.

I realized that, with phrases like the tram is a star, the policeman is a star, I was well on my way towards making dadaistic poetry, that I was attributing such cosmic significance to images observed as reality that every separate noun started whirling through the universe like a meteor. The dada movement was a direct renunciation of God. The universe created by mankind was placed on a level with the divine universe, or even above it.

An explanation was that the World War had given rise to a tremendous disappointment. It took daring to go on. The war had shown what unnatural forces man could make use of without intervention from beyond. Label it pessimism, cynicism, optimism, man's right of absolute self-determination has become an accomplished fact. We are alone. The Creator gave us a vast natural environment, but we are no longer children, we have grown up, and now we have to manage things for ourselves.

No, that image still gives a suggestion of growth, progress. It's too idealistic. Man has always been thrown back on his own resources, ever since he ate from the tree of knowledge. The sweat of his face, the sorrow of bringing forth children were a kind of toll for that freedom. Yet there were ideals to make life bearable. But now sweat and sorrow have become a sombre glory; ideals are no longer necessary and are being cast aside, and now man is faced by the hard task of divesting sweat and pain of their sombreness without being able to reach back to those irrevocably lost ideals. For this is the clearest thing in the crisis: it is a realization of the bankruptcy of our ideals. The economic crisis will pass by, of course; that is to say, at a certain moment a new balance will be struck. A shorter working day, a general obligation to work, a lower standard of living, but with more freedom in the sense of time for oneself, ever faster and more highly mechanized production and distribution under the super-vision of agencies representing ever-growing multitudes – all this will probably be the outcome, and at the same time will reduce the sombreness of sweat and sorrow to an ever-smaller minimum. And no one will yearn for the old over-simple ideals, just as no one, however much admiration he may have for the system, can seriously yearn for the return of Roman law or pyramid-building. But the spiritual aspect of the crisis, the bankruptcy of ideals, is definitive. It is out of the question that things such as religion, beauty, and nature will ever serve again as refuges for any but the introspective individual. Man, the multitude, no longer considers these notions to have any guiding value, and will not change his mind.

If I rightly understand Huizinga's book *In the Shadow of Tomorrow*, he holds the same opinion. He trembles on surveying the bankruptcy. Only of scholarship – to his thinking certainly not the party least guilty of destroying ideals, if there is any question of guilt – only of scholar-ship does he say that it has no recourse other than to go on according to its established method. His 'Diagnosis of the Spiritual Distemper of Our Time,' as the subtitle of the book reads, is extremely apt. The shadow of the future blurs each sharp line. Nowadays everything seems vague, and there is practically nothing that promises a vital future or appears to be rooted at all in solid ground. Our human organization, with its details that function so precisely, sticks together like grains of sand – if one actually still can speak of an organization.

There are still a few master spirits, but no disciples. And what is spirit without disciples? A museum curio and nothing more. We are living in an age of which in all probability everything will disappear, and in which all that is still being created is doomed to death. But that is simply the way things are.

Verse can be of particular importance in a period of crisis. The world is turned upside down. The old order of things is gone for good: that much is certain, everyone admits it, in more or less friendly or covert terms. There will be a new order, a new level, in which the old spaces will give way to spaces constructed by mankind. Man's spirit must be adapted to the products turned out with apparent ease by man's technology. The arts can play an important rôle in this process of adaptation. Poetry must work for the future; that is to say, it must conceive of the future as already existent and so to speak prepare a place in it for the human spirit.

But how can poetry make the world habitable once more? The world is a hell, a desert, for whoever dares open his eyes. Neither the infinitely vast nor the infinitesimally small, the two areas where the imagination takes over the task of the intellect, arouses any interest except in laboratories. The only invention which our age can match against the Parthenon is the motor. I am not an embittered poet. I do not go round with long hair and a corduroy jacket fulminating against my times because my times do not appreciate me and my soul. I have adjusted myself, I am an ordinary human being. I admit that the principle of the motor is as ingenious in conception as the drawing which must have served as a basis for the Parthenon. But I say that the Parthenon has achieved reality once and for all, whereas the motor, though it is perfect as a principle, is dust as material. I have had spells of modernism. Sitting in a cinema, I have been as moved on seeing the skyscrapers of New York in the newsreel as when I first saw the cathedral looming up above the narrow streets of Chartres.

'No,' says an American friend of mine, 'there you're mistaken. The cathedral of Chartres said something to your grandfather and will say the same thing to your grandchildren, but the New York skyscrapers are only built for a shorter or longer period, like temporary buildings for an exposition. We don't build cathedrals in America, we build ruins. The reality is gone, the rhythm that makes matter durable. All right, you say, we make a machine; the machine is dust, but the principle remains and we make a thousand machines. We are living in a world that provides food, clothing, and all the rest for infinitely more people than was ever possible under any earlier economic order. We simply have to pay more attention to the quantity than to the quality. And it doesn't make any difference, because everything can be replaced and copied. In fact, new needs are created: speed, cigarettes. And everything within the means of all.'

'Fine,' says the man with long hair that I actually am, 'I can admire all that, but I want to live. My mind needs to have contact with others, not merely to prowl round in empty imagination. My mind meets no obstacles, it glides through everything like a ghost. I don't feel matter anywhere. I feel dust. Between the urge and its gratification there is no longer any interval to strengthen the urge and ennoble the gratification. When I go walking through the new suburbs built on speculation and long-term leases, I am walking through a house of cards where people eat badly, dress badly, and make love for fear of loneliness. The heart of town that has stood for ages will survive for ages longer than those desperate garden suburbs with their tiny front lawns and coloured floor-lamps. How can poetry make this almost shifting sand habitable?'

Yet it wasn't that easy. Of course you should live in the desert too. But no, no, not yielding, not playing fair weather. No more of art as a consolation, no more using poetry to dupe a half-aroused humanity. Rather than that consider yourself a John the Baptist feeding on locusts and wild honey, clothed with camel's hair, crying in the wilderness, in the belief that someone will come mightier than I, the latchet of whose shoes I am not worthy to unloose. Reduce yourself to the minimum, yet retain a firm faith in order, in numbers, in the universe created by man, formed by his mature hand but still immature spirit. Be like a monk, be like a soldier, constantly with order and discipline in mind, for the moment present only in abstract elation.

I, for my part, made my choice. I decided to study Dutch. I went to another town where I had no sentimental ties, where there was not a memory at every street corner to make me live in the lost tense, and I moved into a working man's house where I had the walls painted white and cut my furnishings to the bare minimum. My chief activities were studying, watering my plants, and throwing bread to seagulls skimming past.

Gradually life became bearable. As I walked through the crowded streets, or sat beside my window in the evening, the multitudes of people began to murmur like a river. I was as elated as a thirsty traveller in the desert when he hears the sound of water. I began to realize that people do not live in the unreal suburban homes dotting the countryside like tents; where people live is in the offices, the factories, the hospitals, the cafés, the stations, everywhere that masses of people gather together. And in research, in pure study, in formulas.

I was at my wits' end how I could combine abstraction and multitude. They seemed as remote from each other as the South Pole and the North. The combination between abstraction and multitude *was* being made, as I could see, but ideologically, with political intentions. Such slogans as nation, race, fatherland became popular as enthusiastic terms over against family, household, birthplace. The circle became somewhat larger as a result, but the term border became all the sharper. It had about as much to do with what I imagined as a formal garden with a forest. No, multitude and abstraction, my two sole sources of elation, either have universal validity or they are illusions. English is the finest language, because it is such a mixture of the Romance and the Germanic. Our whole culture developed along the shores of the Mediterranean, because that inland sea linked three continents together like a navigable market square. National awareness can only be of value as a need to communicate to other nations. Borders, accentuated by ideologies but ever more quickly crossed by new means of transportation, are nowadays difficult to take seriously. They are utterly incompatible with the urge towards spiritual expansion, the human universe.

My thinking found added support when I looked at surrealistic painting and reflected on the possible significance of *neue Sachlichkeit*. It is not for nothing that such a term has become popular. *Neue Sachlichkeit*, or surrealism, for one is the literary term and the other the term in painting for the same principle, think along the following lines, if I am not mistaken. The essence of multitude and abstraction is not depictable. Just as the unconscious, just as the forces of nature are not depictable in themselves. Elation consists only in the awareness of their presence. The effect of their presence is everywhere, no matter where. The perceptible presence in every thing whatsoever of a force of nature, an unconsciousness, a multitude, an abstraction sets the thing in vibration, and this charge makes it into inspired matter, that is to say, beauty. A single leaf from a tree, any leaf, is beautiful, not because of its beautiful form, as people used to say, but because it is a product representative of the woods, the sun and rain, the soil, and the moment. The entire sea waves in every wave, all mankind lives in every man, whoever or however, as long as he does not restrict himself artificially and become enslaved to his individuality. Surrealist paintings with their silence, their unemotional lucidity, their clearly distinguishable objects, as mysterious as they are banal, objects that seem to be arranged in the very universe and whose cool forms seem to indicate where the beginning is of that universe that does not stop inside them (for they themselves are only an edge, a transparent surface) – seeing such paintings, and reading modern prose in which the ordinary run–of–the–mill things that we do automatically, unconcernedly, are treated as of more universal importance than the violent moments of conflict and passion, in which we are usually more than ever the slave of our individual delimitations – this painting and this prose filled me with an intense elation, welling up from both sources, abstraction and multitude, together.

Then I began on my poem *Awater*. Awater was to be an arbitrary individual with whom I had no personal ties. Awater had to be the name for one person, but he was to remain abstraction and multitude. At any cost I had to avoid coming into contact with him, for that is when the weaknesses begin, and thinking about him I noticed that even before I had given him a name I had already begun transferring a great deal of myself into him. No, he must remain a silhouette, a clear, translucent surface. At the outside he might be a travelling companion. I had no examples. I could find some help in the masterly early verses of Jean Cocteau, the French poet, and the American T. S. Eliot. But they, unlike the surrealists, had tended to under-estimate their *métier*, their craft. In search of abstraction and multitude, they had thrown their very verse-form overboard as ballast. I too felt that the emotional verse-form was no longer any good. But for what I wanted I had to search rather for the source than for an extreme. I had already decided to choose an old European form, the form of the *Song of Roland*.

Now that I've started talking about the origins of this poem, there were a few other things that should be mentioned, even though they are of a personal nature. My brother had died in the Indies. My plans for a trip, I was to go and meet him, came to nothing. Suddenly the notion of travelling took on an indeterminate quality. Every turn round the block became a trip. The unfamiliar town became even more wondrous than before.

And I should also tell how I came upon the name

Awater. At first I had another name, the name of a former acquaintance of mine, as a crutch. That name bothered me once the poem began to take shape, because it was so difficult to put aside the image it called up from my memory. A name is a man. One afternoon I was having coffee at a friend's. A doctor whom I had never met before was also there. He said, 'I'll just phone the hospital to see if I can stay a bit longer.' He asked to be connected with a clinic and inquired how the patient Awater was getting along. I can still hear him saying, 'Awater, no, no, Awater.' I immediately decided to use that name.

It would be hard to think of a more fleeting contact than that between me and the man who was called Awater in real life. Only his name, accidentally heard for the first time, obsessed me. The philologists have given ever so much significance to that name. 'A' is the old word for water. Awater is twice water. The water that restores taste to the water. The primeval water. But there are more and deeper meanings in the word. It is also a word in Sanskrit; it is also a monogram of my parents' two given names. And above all it means it–doesn't–matter–which individual, a neighbour, a fellow man representative of the multitude, who has approached me along the sheerest thread of contact.

This, then, is the entire prehistory of the poem. The pursuit of Awater, and the love I developed for him, made the desert habitable, or at least travellable, for me. The journey began in his shadow, but the love did not degenerate into attachment. Rather, it gave me the strength to continue the journey. I hope that something of this comes through in the poem.

Translated by James S. Holmes

Martinus Nijhoff's *Awater* as a Dutch Contribution to Modernism

WILJAN VAN DEN AKKER

The poem *Awater* presents itself as a classical epic, with an invocation in the first section and a final section functioning as peroration. Merely because of the absence of the 'I', the opening and conclusion can be distinguished from the actual 'story'. When the Orient Express chugs into the poem, the 'I' vanishes.

The actual 'story' begins in the second section, with the sentence 'I've seen a man.' The first word fixes the point of view: the story is told by an 'I' who states that he is looking for a travelling companion. His loneliness is caused by the death of his brother, and, as will become clear later on in the poem, that of his mother. He has seen a man, an indiscriminate office-clerk, and decides to follow him for an evening to find out whether he can fulfil the part of travelling companion. Right from the start anonymity is important: 'I've seen a man. He doesn't have a name.' This way the anonymous clerk immediately becomes an enigmatic character. But on a somewhat more realistic level it says: 'I've seen a man, but I don't know the fellow.' Anyone familiar with Modernist texts will know that if an author chooses an 'I' for his protagonist, he creates possibilities for an unreliable point of view and manipulation of the reader. Precisely this is exploited here in order to make the projection as effective as possible. What the reader gets to know about the person of Awater is less than the 'I' purports. For isn't it the 'I' who heavily charges the anonymous gentleman with meaning by ways of projection? Reading on a realistic level again, this means that the scene that describes how hard it is for Awater to keep his mind on his work because he keeps thinking of his mother – 'Oh, Mother, you will never wear the fur / you counted every penny to afford' – is misleading since we share the preoccupations of the speaker, who has no knowledge, and can't have any knowledge, about someone else's thoughts.

This speaker is so obsessed by his longing for a travelling companion that he considers even the simplest actions of the office-clerk to be significant for his project. Reality is transformed by obsession. Awater's somewhat tired look at the end of a working day is perceived in the following way: 'eyes fixed, it seems, on some remote horizon.' And when the clerk glances at a shop-window of a travel agency, his pursuer pounces on the act with the following interpretation: 'It seems he really does intend to travel.'

While the daily movements of an office-clerk are given near-metaphysical proportions, little, in fact, happens. Awater goes to the barber's, afterwards to a café, where he plays a game of chess, and finally descends on a restaurant. Until that moment neither the 'I' nor the reader knows anything definite about this gentleman, who, in turn, is unaware of being tailed and, indeed, of being renamed. In the café the waiter states that he does not know the man and as long as this knowledge is missing, the possibilities of projection are unlimited.

In the restaurant, however, the situation changes. It appears that Awater is well-known there and, moreover, that he is a famous performer, whose life, however, is steeped in mystery – 'Some say he spends his evenings reading Greek, / but others claim it's actually Irish Gaelic.' When invited to do so, the man sings a song, albeit after considerable hesitation. From that moment on he has spoken and the possibility of projection collapses. Slowly but inevitably Awater now shows his true nature. As a result, the 'I', after having left the restaurant, begins to have serious doubts about the sense of the whole undertaking – 'A host of cares and worries spring to mind: / there's post at home, I haven't told the cleaner / that I am leaving on a trip, the window's / open'. The failure of the pursuit is announced unmistakably. At the same time the 'I' even begins to doubt the sense of his prospective journey – 'what do / I think I'm doing going travelling?' The doubt about Awater's suitability reaches a climax in the final scene in the station square. A Salvationist, surrounded by a crowd, holds a mirror up to her audience, offering a solution for the fact that 'We live our lives all wrong', by drawing attention to the Gospel. Awater appears to be fascinated, which is not so surprising as the young woman's promise, 'No one [. . .] has ever loved in vain', contrasts sharply with the sombre words with which Awater concludes *his* song: 'You will not see my face on earth again.' The quest has reached its climax. For the first time Awater turns and there is a direct contact between pursuer and pursued. Reality has gained the final victory over fiction, the projector has overheated and burns out. Awater stands still, this indicating that he finds comfort in a Christian, metaphysical, vertical worldview. The 'I', on the contrary, dashes off at this moment, as fast as 'if I'd seen the train I had to catch.' He doesn't disappear by train, though, but dissolves in the poem, horizontally.

No matter how many interpretative moments my analysis may have known, I have so far considered the surface of the text, and in doing so I have reduced a rich literary work to a mere story. What is this poem about? The question is hard if not impossible to answer. *Awater* provides the reader with a formidable paradox between structure and interpretation, between form and content. The structure of the text is clear: there is no trace of the fragmented prosody so many avant-garde poets between the two World Wars deemed necessary. Quite the contrary: *Awater* has been modelled on a centuries-old text, the mediaeval *Chanson de Roland*, in which the technique of the *laisse-monorime* is used: within one section the final syllable of every line contains a particular vowel, a new vowel being used for a new section. The invocation – 'Be here with me, immortal timeless being / that moves upon the face of nascent waters' – gives the poem a classical opening, in which no reader will fail to recognize the reference to Genesis. The story-line is uncomplicated, at least if one is aware of the manipulation with the unreliable point of view. The setting is ordinary: a modern city with banks, cafés, restaurants, revolving doors, electric lights and fans. Also the language has been adjusted to this setting: colloquial language prevails, as in 'to see, as they say, which way the wind blows'. The intended travelling companion, too, is nothing out of the ordinary, since an office-clerk can be hardly seen as 'poetic', especially not in 1934.

The poem stays close to reality: a modern, twentieth-century city. But this is only half of the story. Time and again the reader is carried back to an age-old, mythical reality, in which the 'timeless being' is invoked, in which Noah builds and Jonah preaches. With the greatest ease reality is mythologized: daily activities are given a mythical interpretation. An example of this can be found in the scene at the barber's, where 'A notice on the door says, Cut and Shave'. An ordinary sign becomes a symbol and, accordingly, something that has to be interpreted. Awater is characterized as an 'iceberg', a metaphor that seems to have been inspired by reality: think of the white cape a barber puts around his clients. But at the same time this metaphor contributes to the mystification of the person of Awater: not only does the comparison apply an aspect of 'icy coldness' to Awater, it also conveys inscrutability: just like an iceberg, more than three fourths of Awater are invisible, and so unknowable. At precisely the moment when the reader thinks he can get a grip on this man, he escapes again. 'I've never seen Awater closer by / than in this mirror'. The reader be warned, a mirror is a perfect reflector, but also a perfect illusion. The smaller the distance becomes, the greater the inscrutability and hence alienation, for 'never has he appeared / so absolutely inaccessible.' It is impossible to get a grip on reality because reality is blown up to mythical proportions. But myth does not offer any stability either because it constantly reverts to everyday reality. Now Awater is connected with Moses, then he is identified with John the Baptist: 'this man who's clad in camel's hair / thread through a needle's eye.' All the time the text offers suggestions and interpretations, without however offering any certainty. Or, to put it in a positive way, the reader is at liberty to interpret the text in more ways than one. And this is exactly what readers *have* done. The name Awater in itself inspired one of them, the major Dutch writer Simon Vestdijk, to devise forty different interpretations.

Even more than the enigmatic character of Awater, the references to other literary works made critics snatch up their pens. I have already pointed out references to Genesis, Moses and John. But there is more. The opening of the poem seems an echo of Milton's *Paradise Lost*, in which the muse is invoked as follows: 'And chiefly Thou O Spirit . . . / Instruct me, for Thou know'st; Thou from the first / Wast present, and with mighty wings outspread / Dove-like satst brooding on the vast Abyss.' And there's still more. 'Whoosh, says the wind, on, on' is a quotation from a fairytale by Hans Christian Andersen. The song Awater sings in the restaurant turns out to be a perfect translation of a sonnet by Petrarch.

The following list of names and titles apparently have found a place in *Awater*: the old French *Song of Roland*, Van Ostaijen, Ovid, Rimbaud, the Pied Piper of Hamelin, three fairytales by Andersen, Gérard de Nerval, Jean Cocteau, James Joyce, the legend of the Holy Grail, Milton, Guillaume Apollinaire, T. S. Eliot, Jules Romains, Oswald Spengler, Jung, Freud, Thomas Mann, Saint John Perse, Marcel Proust, Petrarch and, last but of course not least, the Old and New Testaments.

If we consider this list, we can distinguish four groups. In the first place there is the remarkably small number of Dutch writers. The second group includes men like Freud, Spengler and Jung, of whom one can say that they have influenced every serious writer in Europe. More interesting is the group of contemporary international writers such as Mann, Proust, Cocteau or Eliot, who all fit into the Modernist circle. The rest of the final group includes mythical literature, namely Ovid, the legend of the Holy Grail, the Bible, the *Chanson de Roland*, the Pied Piper of Hamelin and Andersen's fairy world. The problem of alienation is given a modern, contemporary setting, in which an old, mythical reality constantly resonates. This is a distinguishing feature of Modernism; Eliot's *The Waste Land* comes to mind first of all.

Awater deals with man's fundamental alienation in the modern world. The project ends in failure: we are not granted a travelling companion, an ideal alter ego. On a realistic level, the deaths of the brother and mother form the immediate cause of his loneliness; on a symbolic level, however, they indicate that an irreparable breach in time has come about. As the waiter in the café remarks: 'The times [. . .] have changed.' There is no continuum with the past, but only a gap. At the same time there is the awareness that an age-old history time and again repeats itself in different guises, 'For Noah builds, but not an ark. / Jonah preaches, but not at Nineveh'. The poem is a modern quest, a search of modern man in a contemporary setting: the city with the attributes of daily life, including colloquial speech and modern technology. The world has become uninhabitable, a desert, in which one can only give meaning to one's existence by projecting illusions or mythologizing reality. But this also fails: the attempt to lift existential loneliness and heal the breach with the past does not find an adequate basis in reality. Exploring hope for the future results in the finding of present despair.

All these elements firmly anchor *Awater* in international Modernism. And a fascinating aspect of modernist poetry is its fundamental ambiguity, its ambivalence and its openness to many interpretations. *The Waste Land* and *Awater* represent a kind of text whose meaning is not unambiguous, indeed, whose meaning is determined by the point of view of the reader. It seems that not just one individual interpretation, but rather the sum of all of them points in the direction of a meaning.

Modernist Poetics

Awater takes us back to the year 1934. The poet, Martinus Nijhoff, is forty years old, an age when many poets show themselves past masters, and at the same time feel the need to take stock of their efforts. *Awater* is the epic conclusion of Nijhoff's last collection of poems, *Nieuwe Gedichten* (New Poems). He never was a voluminous writer: only two collections preceded this last one. At a time when Symbolism tried to overcome life's schizophrenia in a linguistic, and hence illusory synthesis, the young Nijhoff in 1916 sounded a more gloomy note. His first collection, entitled *De Wandelaar* (The Wanderer) demonstrates life's fundamental duality in its full magnitude, without, however, trying to escape it in any way. Quite the contrary, for Nijhoff was aware 'of standing naked in a chaotic world, with neither a transcendental roof over his head, nor a vestigial trust in the power of reason.'

Eight years later, in 1924, Nijhoff establishes himself as a major poet once and for all, with the volume *Vormen* (Forms). But major does not necessarily mean popular. Contemporary readers were having trouble with his poetry and wondered whether they were dealing with a poet who couples a rich variety of emotions with intellectual acumen – or rather someone who takes in his readers by plucking their heart strings by means of his linguistic ingenuity. Technique or emotion? Play or real? Form or content? Language or reality?

Ten years later, in 1934, the year of *Awater*, we find ourselves in the midst of a worldwide crisis, which not only delivered a serious economic blow, but also brought about an awareness of lost idealism. With the exception of a few avant-garde movements, such as Italian Futurism for example, poetry and politics had been avowed opponents for decades. And while unemployment increasingly resulted in grinding poverty, most Dutch readers and critics still viewed poetry as a 'spontaneous overflow of powerful feelings', as Wordsworth put it, and if they had passed that stage, they looked for the solution the Symbolists could offer.

In the twenties and thirties, Nijhoff time and again resisted an expressive poetics, the Romantic tendency to highlight the relationship between poet and poem, to identify poetry as a reflection of the emotions of its maker. Modernist poets attempted to change this set of ideas. The most important change was the shift in attention from reality to language. By way of the discovery that language does not reflect reality straightforwardly, they reached the insight that language is an autonomous instrument, something that *creates* a world rather than imitates one. Constant resistance to the Romantic conception, or the legacy of Romanticism, is typical of Modernist poetics. Modernists contrast the poet as the unacknowledged legislator of the world, with the poet as craftsman, someone who knows how to handle language rather than ideas. Inspiration gives way to craftsmanship. In the words of the German poet Gottfried Benn, 'a poem hardly ever comes into being, a poem is *made*.' To quote Nijhoff, who gave the following advice to a young writer: 'write every day at a fixed time, as a test that you are able to cope with every form of disgust or inspiration.

The rest will come all by itself.' As for Valéry, inspiration is something the reader thinks the writer had.

Technical skill distinguishes the major poet from the minor one, not the quality or quantity of ideas. Degas, the famous French painter, also wrote sonnets; he was a friend of Stephane Mallarmé and once called on him for his help. 'I can't seem to be able to complete this little poem,' he moaned to the great master, 'I don't understand it: I'm bursting with ideas.' 'But my dear Degas', came the razor-sharp reply, 'poems aren't written with ideas but with words.' Auden once formulated it even more wittily: '"Why do you want to write poetry?" If the young man answers: "I have important things I want to say," then he is *not* a poet. If he answers: "I like hanging around words, listening to what they say," then maybe he is *going* to be a poet.'

These ideas caused the poem to be seen as an autonomous linguistic structure that has to travel under its own steam, without the possibility of an appeal to the intentions of its maker. Indeed, the maker declared that the meaning of the poem would only unfold itself after it had been completed. In the words of Auden: 'How can I know what I mean, until I see what I say.'

The above is only a small selection from the set of ideas Modernist poets have expounded in essays, criticism and lectures with unfailing energy. Doing so they formed a circle in which the composer Stravinsky felt as much at home as the French poet Valéry, the Anglo-American T. S. Eliot, the German Benn or Rilke, or the Dutch Nijhoff. And I'd like to dwell on these two. Comparing the critical statements of Eliot and Nijhoff, one finds striking similarities. Both poets have pointed out unremittingly that poetry is not be equated with personal emotions. According to Eliot, 'Poetry is not a turning loose of emotion, but an escape from emotion.' In the words of Nijhoff: 'Keep your heart away from the poem. Poets don't weep.' To Nijhoff, a second-rate writer lets the person die so that the artist can live. But a first-rate writer lets the artist die so that the poem can live. You can hear the shift from maker to what is made. Eliot described it the following way: 'The progress of an artist is a continual self-sacrifice, a continual extinction of personality.' In one of his most beautiful essays, *De Pen op Papier* (The Pen on Paper), in which Nijhoff presents his Modernist credentials, he advises himself to 'only write about the feelings of others. If this goes too slowly, keep a diary, and whenever it happens that you are paying attention to your own feelings, write down what comes to your mind, and do so with the utmost daring, exaggeration, literary lust and self-pity. When you turn to verse, however, only the feelings of others. For instance, there's something wrong with some bond of love: put down your own state of mind in the diary, but try to express the attitude and pain of your girlfriend in a poem.'

As I pointed out before, most Modernists declared that the making of a poem is not merely a search for an adequate form, but especially an exploration of content. 'And what is the experience that the poet is so bursting to communicate?' Eliot wondered in one of his Norton lectures delivered at Harvard University. 'By the time it has settled down into a poem it may be so different from the original experience as to be hardly recognisable. What is to be communicated was not in existence before the poem was completed.' I'll let his Dutch colleague reply to this: 'Writing, one starts to write. A thought becomes a word, the words continue the thought. Even a little writing gives more inspiration than a lot of thinking.' The poet only accepts responsibility for the composition of the poem, not for the final meaning of it.

Seen in this perspective, the notion of autonomy can also be understood as a metaphor for the wish to have a poem generate meanings in the readers as a result of a built-in quality: ambiguity. Autonomy is a form of denial: poetry is anti-mimetic, anti-expressive, anti-romantic, anti-pragmatic, anti-inspirational, anti-emotional etc. It is remarkable that Modernists tend to explain what poetry is *not*, rather than clarify what it *is*. Many definitions have been negatively formulated. It says: 'Poetry is *not* a turning loose of emotion', and then, following the coordinating *but*, 'an *escape* from emotion', which is again a negative. So autonomy can also be seen as a kind of ideology: poets analyse the past with sharp eyes, but refuse to give a picture of the future. Modernists tend to formulate the characteristics of a work in terms of the creative process that precedes it, rather than in terms of its function or of the world it evokes.

To put things differently, the resistance to Romantic poetics required a new mode of writing. One of the fundamental qualities of the poem, namely its ambiguity, can be related to the idea that its maker does not claim the authority to know better than anyone else what the text means. On the contrary, the poet has finally become the reader of his own text. According to Eliot, 'a poet knows what he was meaning to mean. But what a poem means is as much what it means to others as what it means to the author.' Having completed a poem, Eliot tells it without any mercy: 'Go away! Find a place for yourself in a book – and don't expect *me* to take any further interest in you.' A similar attitude was displayed by Nijhoff, in a lecture he delivered in 1935, one year after *Awater* had been published. He revealed that poems grow very slowly: 'I go about with poems, or rather beginnings of poems, for years, sometimes six years, while the poem builds up gradually, sometimes with a word, sometimes with a line. I am a kind of coral reef, which grows by fits and starts. When such a poem is finished, it doesn't have anything more to say.' The poem will have to be able to stand all by itself. In the words of Nijhoff: 'Once a poem is good, its interpretation is limitless.' Nijhoff never denied *or* confirmed any of the suggested interpretations; he took all of them seriously. When a critic traced the etymology of the word Awater to Sanskrit, Nijhoff wrote: 'Although I don't know any Sanskrit, that doesn't mean you are wrong.'

It is this tradition, the tradition of autonomy, which turned out to be very influential on Dutch poetry, even after 1940. The poetry of Gerrit Kouwenaar, Hans Faverey or even Rutger Kopland cannot be understood without it.

An emotional cryptogram with infinite meanings

And thus we return to where we started, the poem *Awater*, which has served all the purposes of its maker. Whereas Eliot's *The Waste Land* gets the international trophy for the most commented-upon twentieth-century poem, *Awater* deserves the national prize of the Low Countries. No matter how simple the text may seem at first glance, readers have found the poem extremely difficult. Its first readers, in particular, did not know what to do, since much of the poem was at right angles with the conception most people had of poetry. A totally new register was used, and as so often in art, the breaking of conventions was initially understood to be a failure. Not only was *Awater* banal in its use of language and imagery, it was also hard to understand, hermetic. Initially, ambiguity provoked irritation, which translated into a reproach directed at the maker, formulated as dishonesty, coquetry or lack of emotions, as so many Modernist poets (and artists) have experienced. The reader prefers clarity, and not something which at first glance looks firm and tempting, but which on closer investigation slips through one's fingers and which on repeated sampling leaves a taste of water. However, what in those first years of the poem's reception was referred to as unclarity, has gradually come to be recognized as a fascinating mystery that provokes thought and written comments. Critics no longer battled with the text, but with each other, competing for the honour of the one and only true interpretation. If one keeps some distance from this quarrel, one soon realizes that no one can or should be granted a patent on the true interpretation. At precisely the moment when one critic thinks he has won the argument once and for all, the case is re-opened from an unexpected angle. It is a suit without a judge, a plea without a jury, a trial without a verdict.

As I have stated before, the many references to other literary works made critics rush to their typewriters. Although this may sound rather ironic, things were somewhat easier for the reader of *The Waste Land* in this respect. For Eliot soon after its first publication added several pages of notes to the text. Although it has become clear by now that he didn't reveal all of his sources, he did mark the kind of attitude the reader was to assume with regard to the text. Eliot cherished an 'unpoetic' attitude towards his audience: after all, he hadn't put in the notes to explain the text, for, as he said, the poem could very well explain itself, but rather because his publisher had wanted to pad out the volume. This is a striking demonstration of the fact that a poet, even when putting on the mask of seriousness and honesty, never ceases to play a role in his own circus. He sometimes makes a generous gesture and invites the Ladies and Gentlemen for a peep behind the scenes: he mentions his sources, he gives away the secret of his method or informs us of his 'underlying intentions'. The listener or reader feels caught up in the circle of the initiated and doesn't realize that all this is part of the show. He has been shown around by a real ringmaster, who shows but little resemblance to the man who, after the performance, removes his top hat and counts the box-office receipts of the evening.

Although Nijhoff has never added any notes to his poem, he can rival Eliot in providing clarity by putting up smoke screens. In the 1935 lecture, which was found in manuscript after his death, Nijhoff *himself* seemed to have pointed out his literary sources, thus putting his readers on the track of intertextuality. But no matter how much Nijhoff may have divulged, it appears that he didn't tell his audience that the song Awater sings in the restaurant is a faithful translation of a sonnet by Petrarch. What is withheld is sometimes more informative than what is disclosed. Of the authors Nijhoff has drawn upon most heavily for the composition of *Awater*, he discusses Proust and Lawrence at greatest length. Further down in the manuscript James Joyce and Virginia Woolf join the list, although only in a passing reference.

What should one conclude from this? Firstly, that

Nijhoff mentioned four novelists, and not one single poet. Secondly, that all four of them belong to the core of international Modernism. And finally that he decided to refer to Joyce in passing, and this while it is precisely *Ulysses* that is frequently echoed in *Awater*.

I've just said that there was no poet on Nijhoff's list, but that's not entirely correct. Nijhoff states that he couldn't find good examples in this genre. This is what he has to say about Eliot: 'T. S. Eliot was of some use to me. But he thought too little of his métier, his profession. He smashed his verse form like a window. I, too, felt that the emotional verse form was no longer suitable. But, for what I wanted, I searched for origin, rather than for extreme. I had already decided to choose an old European form, the form of the *Song of Roland*.' On the one hand Nijhoff indicates that Eliot aspires after a similar goal in his poetry, but on the other hand he finds Eliot unsuitable as an example since he didn't take tradition into account. Nijhoff's judgment is superficial and, moreover, incorrect if one considers that already in 1917 Eliot had taken a stand against the supposed freedom of free verse and in 1919 published his famous essay *Tradition and the Individual Talent*. Nijhoff knew that. Judging by the text of Nijhoff's lecture, there can be no question about his being familiar with Eliot's work in 1935. But leaving aside this manuscript, the reader of Nijhoff's complete works would conclude that this poet got to know his Anglo-American colleague only at the end of his life. In the more than a thousand pages of essays and criticism, Eliot's name comes up only once, namely in a review of *The Cocktail Party*, dating from 1952, one year before Nijhoff died. Again: what is withheld has to be significant. 'There is something here of the phenomenon of citing all sources, except the one to which you really owe most'. This is a quotation from Geoffrey Hough, concerning Eliot, but it could have equally been made for Nijhoff.

The two poets in a sense resemble each other. Both were respectable gentlemen, who, for their day, behaved rather 'unpoetically', that is to say, in an intellectual way; time and again both emphatically separated poetry from personal emotion and both were masters of technique and writers of a small body of work. Also Eliot liked to fool his critics by sending them off in the wrong direction. In 1961, just before *his* death, when he had already completed his oeuvre, Eliot admitted he had been influenced most by Jules Laforgue. But during his active years as a poet, Eliot never dedicated a single essay to this Frenchman. 'Eliot has often taken a mischievous pleasure in sending his critics to bark upon the wrong tree', as Geoffrey Hough put it.

Let me now cite a few parallels-in-contrast between *Awater* and *The Waste Land*. In the motto of *Awater* one can hear the counterpart of the motto of *The Waste Land*: 'Wanted: a travelling companion' can be contrasted with the words of the Sibyl, in which she expresses her wish: 'I want to die.' The second section of Eliot's poem, entitled 'A game of chess', has its parallel in the game of chess Awater plays in the café. A few more details: when Awater is in the restaurant, the poem says: 'A single snowflake swirls through drops of blood', in which line one can read a reference to the legend of the Holy Grail, taking the form of a reversed quotation, a technique which often occurs in Modernist texts. The same Grail-legend forms one of the sub-texts of *The Waste Land*. The 'ruins' at the beginning of *Awater* – 'debris' is not an adequate translation of the Dutch word 'puinhopen'; 'ruins' would be better – bring to mind the 'fragments I have shored against my ruins' at the end of Eliot's poem.

At another level, stepping back from the texts, it can be observed that the game of literary allusions plays a conspicuous part in both poems. However, Nijhoff wouldn't be Nijhoff if he hadn't gone beyond imitation. Four important motifs from *The Waste Land* return in *Awater*, namely the woman, the desert, the city and the water, but they are projected differently, seen with back-lighting. In his poem Eliot more than once consults Dante, preferably quoting from *Inferno* and once or twice from *Purgatorio*, but never from *Paradiso*, at least if we can rely on the notes the poet added himself. Apparently, the dark side of life was more appealing to Eliot, and purgatory was the best conceivable light. That Nijhoff chose precisely the Renaissance poet Petrarch, who was more involved with man than with God, and borrowed not just a few lines but a whole sonnet from him, shows how one master wanted to correct the other and rival him. The two texts mirror each other, up to and including the titles: the 'water' in *Awater* opposes the 'land' in *The Waste Land*.

I would even go one step further and present a daring question: who would come to mind from the following description? A respectable gentleman, clean-shaven and working at an office; who is also known to be a great artist, surrounded however by mystery; who sings a song which at first hearing seems to be an emotional outpour-ing, but which on reflection turns out to be a translation; it says of him that 'The meaning of his cries is lost to all' and 'It's wilderness where he lifts up his arms'; he was last seen in a square in 1934, listening to a Salvationist, indi-cating that he has resorted to Christianity.

At the end of Nijhoff's quest, in the square where the Salvationist advises the bystanders to direct their hopes upwards, the two *dramatis personae* for the first time look each other in the eye. Two poets meet, but they opt for diverging roads. The Englishman primarily depicts the world as a barren desert, a waste land; he chooses a highly fragmented verse form for this, but eventually takes refuge in a Christian, vertical direction. When *Awater* was written it had been well known that Eliot had publicly turned to Christianity. His Dutch colleague lets a more optimistic sound predominate, he chooses a more closed, tighter verse form and takes refuge in a secular, horizontal direction. Both, however, come up with hermetic texts, which provide no answer as to the outcome of the whole undertaking. After the quest has foundered in front of the station at midnight, the 'I' as protagonist disappears to give way to a more neutral, general narrator. After this failure the reader expects a conclusion, an extended hand. But what applies to Modernist texts in general also applies to *Awater*: it tells us in detail what is *not* possible, rather than showing us what *can* be done. At the moment things ought to start, the poem ends. By the time the train leaves and the journey must begin, we have reached the very last line and can't go along. It is as if the curtain goes *up* at the end of the performance, without the audience being given a chance to see whether there is anything to see. All evening we have been watching a performance that eventually turns out to be a prologue. The Orient Express seems the secular solution to and substitute for lost metaphysics. It is the new deity, the God of technology. But where does it lead mankind? Does the train represent a glorification of life without divine guidance, or is it the personification of complete desertion? The Orient Express is 'single-minded', 'she doesn't care; she's even immune'. 'She moves and leaves at the appointed hour', but where to is unclear. Or perhaps it is more apt to say that after this prologue the reader may write the actual play himself. The writer withdraws at the climax of the plot, just as Hans Castorp in Thomas Mann's *Der Zauberberg* (The Magic Mountain) is deserted by his author and Jozef K. in Kafka's *Der Prozess* (The Trial) doesn't know whether he is guilty or innocent. And Eliot's reader, after the 'fragments I have shored against my ruins' is left in uncertainty, denoted by the words: 'Shantih shantih shantih.'

The poetics of Nijhoff can become richer when viewed in the light of international Modernism. The mythical undercurrent, the incorporation of literature in literature, the city, alienation, the idea that times have changed while at the same time an age-old history is repeating itself, the use of modern technology as a store of metaphors, the open ending and ambiguity, the autonomy that lies behind the seeming simplicity, the manipulation of the point of view, the highly observing nature, the notion of the victim, or the notion of detachment: all of these are properties of literary Modernism. Yet the phrasing of it all is not so sharp, not so fragmented. The city is not the London Eliot had in mind, with its pollution and poverty. The city in Nijhoff's poem is a village compared to Eliot's London or Alfred Döblin's Berlin or John Dos Passos's New York. This is related to the Dutch situation: Utrecht (for this is the city where the poem is staged) or Amsterdam still are villages with a touch of a cosmopolitan atmosphere.

Awater is a Dutch contribution to the movement that has produced so many masterpieces between the two

World Wars. And, like all masterpieces, it is rooted in a tradition, it carries on a debate with the most important of its contemporaries in which it has secured a place of its own, a place which is determined by its unique structure and different national perspective. Nijhoff has taken to heart the words of Eliot, who said that 'the historical sense compels a man to write not merely with his own generation in his bones, but with a feeling that the whole of the literatures of Europe from Homer and within it the whole of the literature of his own country has a simultaneous existence and composes a simultaneous order.'

Contributors

WILJAN VAN DEN AKKER (born in 1954) completed his studies in 1986 at Utrecht University with a dissertation on Martinus Nijhoff. He was appointed as full professor of Modern Dutch Literature at Utrecht University in 1987. He was the director of the Research Institute for History and Culture (OGC) from 1994 to 2003 and was the director of institutes at the Royal Academy for Arts and Sciences (KNAW) in Amsterdam from 2003 to 2006. He is now a distinguished professor for Modern Dutch Literature and the Dean of Humanities at Utrecht University. He has also taught in Berlin, Paris and Berkeley. His special field is modernist poetry in an international context. Van den Akker has published a number of books on Nijhoff and is widely considered one of the main authorities on Nijhoff's poetry and poetics.

DAVID COLMER was born in Adelaide in 1960 and, in the early 1990s, settled in Amsterdam where he learned Dutch and became a literary translator. He has translated *Familieziek* by Adriaan van Dis (*Repatriated*, Heinemann, 2008), poems by Anna Enquist (*The Fire Was Here*, Toby Press, 2003) and Gerbrand Bakker's *Boven is het stil* (*The Twin*, Harvill Secker, 2008), among others. This last title was included in the shortlist for the American Best Translated Book Award 2010. Colmer has previously won the biennial New South Wales Premier's Translation Prize and the PEN Trophy, and has twice been awarded the David Reid Poetry Translation Prize. In addition, he has been nominated for the Oxford-Weidenfeld Translation Prize. Colmer's own novels and stories are published by the Dutch publishing company, Contact.

JAMES S. HOLMES was a poet and translator who was born in Collins, Iowa, in 1924 and died in Amsterdam in 1986. He published many highly praised translations, including the standard anthology *Dutch Interior: Postwar Poetry from the Netherlands and Flanders* (Columbia UP, 1984). At the University of Amsterdam he played a crucial role in developing (theoretical) translation studies into a fully-fledged educational programme. It was only from the end of the 1970s onward that he had his own poems published, under his own name and under the pseudonyms 'Jim Holmes' and 'Jacob Lowland'. A salient detail: in 1956, Holmes was the first non-Dutch winner of the Martinus Nijhoff Prize, the principal Dutch literary award in the domain of literary translation.

THOMAS MÖHLMANN (born in 1975) read Modern Dutch Literature at the University of Amsterdam. He is the poetry specialist at the Dutch Foundation for Literature, chief editor of the Dutch poetry magazine *Awater* and editor of several literary websites and poetry anthologies, including *Dit zijn de daden waar ik mens voor was* (Selected Poems of Martinus Nijhoff; Prometheus, Amsterdam, 2008). His first collection of poems, *De vloeibare jongen* (The Liquid Boy; Prometheus, Amsterdam 2005) was shortlisted for the C. Buddingh' Prize for new Dutch-language poetry and was awarded the Lucy B. & C. W. van der Hoogt Prize. In 2009 his second collection, *Kranen open* (Taps Open; Prometheus, Amsterdam) was shortlisted for the Jo Peters Poetry Prize.

DAAN VAN DER VAT was a Dutch poet, writer, journalist and translator. He was born in Groningen in 1909 and studied English Language and Literature in Groningen, Copenhagen and London. He subsequently worked for several years as an English teacher in the Netherlands prior to moving to London as correspondent for *De Tijd*. Between 1945 and 1967 his reports in this daily newspaper appeared under his own name. At the same time, under the pseudonym 'Daan Zonderland', he also published the works that made him famous in the Netherlands: a series of children's books and a plethora of nonsense rhymes and light verse. He died in a hospital near The Hague ten years after his return to the Netherlands. His Collected Poems were published by the Dutch publisher Bert Bakker in 2007.